RESUMES  FOR

SOCIAL SERVICE
CAREERS

THIRD EDITION

RESUMES FOR

SOCIAL SERVICE

CAREERS

The Editors of McGraw-Hill

New York   Chicago   San Francisco   Lisbon   London   Madrid   Mexico City
Milan   New Delhi   San Juan   Seoul   Singapore   Sydney   Toronto

Library of Congress Cataloging-in-Publication Data

Resumes for social service careers : with sample cover letters / the editors of McGraw-Hill.—3rd ed.

p.   cm.

ISBN 0-07-146781-5 (pbk. : alk. paper)

1. Human services—Vocational guidance.   2. Resumes (Employment)   I. McGraw-Hill Companies.

HV10.5.V49   2007

650.14'2—dc22   2006044908

1 2 3 4 5 6 7 8 9 10 11 12 13 14 15 QPD/QPD   0 9 8 7 6

ISBN-13: 978-0-07-146781-0

ISBN-10:   0-07-146781-5

McGraw-Hill books are available at special quantity discounts to use as premiums and sales promotions, or for use in corporate training programs. For more information, please write to the Director of Special Sales, Professional Publishing, McGraw-Hill, Two Penn Plaza, New York, NY 10121-2298. Or contact your local bookstore.

Contents

Introduction

Your resume is a piece of paper (or an electronic document) that serves to introduce you to the people who will eventually hire you. To write a thoughtful resume, you must thoroughly assess your personality, your accomplishments, and the skills you have acquired. The act of composing and submitting a resume also requires you to carefully consider the company or individual that might hire you. What are they looking for, and how can you meet their needs? This book shows you how to organize your personal information and experience into a concise and well-written resume, so that your qualifications and potential as an employee will be understood easily and quickly by a complete stranger.

Writing the resume is just one step in what can be a daunting job-search process, but it is an important element in the chain of events that will lead you to your new position. While you are probably a talented, bright, and charming person, your resume may not reflect these qualities. A poorly written resume can get you nowhere; a well-written resume can land you an interview and potentially a job. A good resume can even lead the interviewer to ask you questions that will allow you to talk about your strengths and highlight the skills you can bring to a prospective employer. Even a person with very little experience can find a good job if he or she is assisted by a thoughtful and polished resume.

Lengthy, typewritten resumes are a thing of the past. Today, employers do not have the time or the patience for verbose documents; they look for tightly composed, straightforward, action-based resumes. Although a one-page resume is the norm, a two-page resume may be warranted if you have had extensive job experience or have changed careers and truly need the space to properly position yourself. If, after careful editing, you still need more than one page to present yourself, it's acceptable to use a second page. A crowded resume that's hard to read would be the worst of your choices.

Distilling your work experience, education, and interests into such a small space requires preparation and thought. This book takes you step-by-step through the process of crafting an effective resume that will stand out in today's competitive marketplace. It serves as a workbook and a place to write down your experiences, while also including the techniques you'll need to pull all the necessary elements together. In the following pages, you'll find many examples of resumes that are specific to your area of interest. Study them for inspiration and find what appeals to you. There are a variety of ways to organize and present your information; inside, you'll find several that will be suitable to your needs. Good luck landing the job of your dreams!

Chapter 1

The Elements of an Effective Resume

An effective resume is composed of information that employers are most interested in knowing about a prospective job applicant. This information is conveyed by a few essential elements. The following is a list of elements that are found in most resumes—some essential, some optional. Later in this chapter, we will further examine the role of each of these elements in the makeup of your resume.

- Heading
- Objective and/or Keyword Section
- Work Experience
- Education
- Honors
- Activities
- Certificates and Licenses
- Publications
- Professional Memberships
- Special Skills
- Personal Information
- References

The first step in preparing your resume is to gather information about yourself and your past accomplishments. Later you will refine this information, rewrite it using effective language, and organize it into an attractive layout. But first, let's take a look at each of these important elements individually so you can judge their appropriateness for your resume.

Heading

Although the heading may seem to be the simplest section of your resume, be careful not to take it lightly. It is the first section your prospective employer will see, and it contains the information she or he will need to contact you. At the very least, the heading must contain your name, your home address, and, of course, a phone number where you can be reached easily.

In today's high-tech world, many of us have multiple ways that we can be contacted. You may list your e-mail address if you are reasonably sure the employer makes use of this form of communication. Keep in mind, however, that others may have access to your e-mail messages if you send them from an account provided by your current company. If this is a concern, do not list your work e-mail address on your resume. If you are able to take calls at your current place of business, you should include your work number, because most employers will attempt to contact you during typical business hours.

If you have voice mail or a reliable answering machine at home or at work, list its number in the heading and make sure your greeting is professional and clear. Always include at least one phone number in your heading, even if it is a temporary number, where a prospective employer can leave a message.

You might have a dozen different ways to be contacted, but you do not need to list all of them. Confine your numbers or addresses to those that are the easiest for the prospective employer to use and the simplest for you to retrieve.

Objective

When seeking a specific career path, it is important to list a job or career objective on your resume. This statement helps employers know the direction you see yourself taking, so they can determine whether your goals are in line with those of their organization and the position available. Normally, an objective is one to two sentences long. Its contents will vary depending on your career field, goals, and personality. The objective can be specific or general, but it should always be to the point. See the sample resumes in this book for examples.

If you are planning to use this resume online, or you suspect your potential employer is likely to scan your resume, you will want to include a "keyword" in the objective. This allows a prospective employer, searching hundreds of resumes for a specific skill or position objective, to locate the keyword and find your resume. In essence, a keyword is what's "hot" in your particular field at a given time. It's a buzzword, a shorthand way of getting a particular message across at a glance. For example, if you are a lawyer, your objective might state your desire to work in the area of corporate litigation. In this case, someone searching for the keyword "corporate litigation" will pull up your resume and know that you want to plan, research, and present cases at trial on behalf of the corporation. If your objective states that you "desire a challenging position in systems design," the keyword is "systems design," an industry-specific shorthand way of saying that you want to be involved in assessing the need for, acquiring, and implementing high-technology systems. These are keywords and every industry has them, so it's becoming more and more important to include a few in your resume. (You may need to conduct additional research to make sure you know what keywords are most likely to be used in your desired industry, profession, or situation.)

There are many resume and job-search sites online. Like most things in the online world, they vary a great deal in quality. Use your discretion. If you plan to apply for jobs online or advertise your availability this way, you will want to design a scannable resume. This type of resume uses a format that can be easily scanned into a computer and added to a database. Scanning allows a prospective employer to use keywords to quickly review each applicant's experience and skills, and (in the event that there are many candidates for the job) to keep your resume for future reference.

Many people find that it is worthwhile to create two or more versions of their basic resume. You may want an intricately designed resume on high-quality paper to mail or hand out *and* a resume that is designed to be scanned into a computer and saved on a database or an online job site. You can even create a resume in ASCII text to e-mail to prospective employers. For further information, you may wish to refer to the *Guide to Internet Job Searching*, by Frances Roehm and Margaret Dikel, updated and published every other year by McGraw-Hill. This excellent book contains helpful and detailed information about formatting a resume for Internet use. To get you started, in Chapter 3 we have included a list of things to keep in mind when creating electronic resumes.

Although it is usually a good idea to include an objective, in some cases this element is not necessary. The goal of the objective statement is to provide the employer with an idea of where you see yourself going in the field. However, if you are uncertain of the exact nature of the job you seek, including an objective that is too specific could result in your not being considered for a host of perfectly acceptable positions. If you decide not to use an objective heading in your resume, you should definitely incorporate the information that would be conveyed in the objective into your cover letter.

Work Experience

Work experience is arguably the most important element of them all. Unless you are a recent graduate or former homemaker with little or no relevant work experience, your current and former positions will provide the central focus of the resume. You will want this section to be as complete and carefully constructed as possible. By thoroughly examining your work experience, you can get to the heart of your accomplishments and present them in a way that demonstrates and highlights your qualifications.

If you are just entering the workforce, your resume will probably focus on your education, but you should also include information on your work or volunteer experiences. Although you will have less information about work experience than a person who has held multiple positions or is advanced in his or her career, the amount of information is not what is most important in this section. How the information is presented and what it says about you as a worker and a person are what really count.

As you create this section of your resume, remember the need for accuracy. Include all the necessary information about each of your jobs, including your job title, dates of employment, name of your employer, city, state, responsibilities, special projects you handled, and accomplishments. Be sure to list only accomplishments for which you were directly responsible. And don't be alarmed if you haven't participated in or worked on special projects, because this section may not be relevant to certain jobs.

The most common way to list your work experience is in *reverse chronological order*. In other words, start with your most recent job and work your way backward. This way, your prospective employer sees your current (and often most important) position before considering your past employment. Your most recent position, if it's the most important in terms of responsibilities and relevance to the job for which you are applying, should also be the one that includes the most information as compared to your previous positions.

Even if the work itself seems unrelated to your proposed career path, you should list any job or experience that will help sell your talents. If you were promoted or given greater responsibilities or commendations, be sure to mention the fact.

The following worksheet is provided to help you organize your experiences in the working world. It will also serve as an excellent resource to refer to when updating your resume in the future.

WORK EXPERIENCE

Job One:

Job Title _____

Dates _____

Employer _____

City, State _____

Major Duties _____

_____

_____

_____

_____

_____

_____

_____

_____

_____

Special Projects _____

_____

_____

_____

Accomplishments _____

_____

_____

_____

_____

_____

Job Two:

Job Title _____

Dates _____

Employer _____

City, State _____

Major Duties _____

_____

_____

_____

_____

_____

_____

_____

Special Projects _____

_____

_____

_____

Accomplishments _____

_____

_____

_____

_____

_____

_____

_____

Job Three:

Job Title _____

Dates _____

Employer _____

City, State _____

Major Duties _____

_____

_____

_____

_____

_____

_____

_____

Special Projects _____

_____

_____

_____

Accomplishments _____

_____

_____

_____

_____

_____

_____

_____

_____

Job Four:

Job Title _____

Dates _____

Employer _____

City, State _____

Major Duties _____

_____

_____

_____

_____

_____

_____

_____

Special Projects _____

_____

_____

_____

Accomplishments _____

_____

_____

_____

_____

_____

_____

_____

Education

Education is usually the second most important element of a resume. Your educational background is often a deciding factor in an employer's decision to interview you. Highlight your accomplishments in school as much as you did those accomplishments at work. If you are looking for your first professional job, your education or life experience will be your greatest asset because your related work experience will be minimal. In this case, the education section becomes the most important means of selling yourself.

Include in this section all the degrees or certificates you have received; your major or area of concentration; all of the honors you earned; and any relevant activities you participated in, organized, or chaired. Again, list your most recent schooling first. If you have completed graduate-level work, begin with that and work your way back through your undergraduate education. If you have completed college, you generally should not list your high-school experience; do so only if you earned special honors, you had a grade point average that was much better than the norm, or this was your highest level of education.

If you have completed a large number of credit hours in a subject that may be relevant to the position you are seeking but did not obtain a degree, you may wish to list the hours or classes you completed. Keep in mind, however, that you may be asked to explain why you did not finish the program. If you are currently in school, list the degree, certificate, or license you expect to obtain and the projected date of completion.

The following worksheet will help you gather the information you need for this section of your resume.

EDUCATION

School One _____

Major or Area of Concentration _____

Degree _____

Dates _____

School Two _____

Major or Area of Concentration _____

Degree _____

Dates _____

Honors

If you include an honors section in your resume, you should highlight any awards, honors, or memberships in honorary societies that you have received. (You may also incorporate this information into your education section.) Often, the honors are academic in nature, but this section also may be used for special achievements in sports, clubs, or other school activities. Always include the name of the organization awarding the honor and the date(s) received. Use the following worksheet to help you gather your information.

HONORS

Honor One _____

Awarding Organization _____

Date(s) _____

Honor Two _____

Awarding Organization _____

Date(s) _____

Honor Three _____

Awarding Organization _____

Date(s) _____

Honor Four _____

Awarding Organization _____

Date(s) _____

Honor Five _____

Awarding Organization _____

Date(s) _____

Activities

Perhaps you have been active in different organizations or clubs; often an employer will look at such involvement as evidence of initiative, dedication, and good social skills. Examples of your ability to take a leading role in a group should be included on a resume, if you can provide them. The activities section of your resume should present neighborhood and community activities, volunteer positions, and so forth. In general, you may want to avoid listing any organization whose name indicates the race, creed, sex, age, marital status, sexual orientation, or nation of origin of its members because this could expose you to discrimination. Use the following worksheet to list the specifics of your activities.

ACTIVITIES

Organization/Activity   _____

Accomplishments   _____

_____

_____

Organization/Activity _____

Accomplishments   _____

_____

_____

Organization/Activity   _____

Accomplishments   _____

_____

_____

As your work experience grows through the years, your school activities and honors will carry less weight and be emphasized less in your resume. Eventually, you will probably list only your degree and any major honors received. As time goes by, your job performance and the experience you've gained become the most important elements in your resume, which should change to reflect this.

Certificates and Licenses

If your chosen career path requires specialized training, you may already have certificates or licenses. You should list these if the job you are seeking requires them and you, of course, have acquired them. If you have applied for a license but have not yet received it, use the phrase "application pending."

License requirements vary by state. If you have moved or are planning to relocate to another state, check with that state's board or licensing agency for all licensing requirements.

Always make sure that all of the information you list is completely accurate. Locate copies of your certificates and licenses, and check the exact date and name of the accrediting agency. Use the following worksheet to organize the necessary information.

CERTIFICATES AND LICENSES

Name of License _____

Licensing Agency _____

Date Issued _____

Name of License _____

Licensing Agency _____

Date Issued _____

Name of License _____

Licensing Agency _____

Date Issued _____

Publications

Some professions strongly encourage or even require that you publish. If you have written, coauthored, or edited any books, articles, professional papers, or works of a similar nature that pertain to your field, you will definitely want to include this element. Remember to list the date of publication and the publisher's name, and specify whether you were the sole author or a coauthor. Book, magazine, or journal titles are generally italicized, while the titles of articles within a larger publication appear in quotes. (Check with your reference librarian for more about the appropriate way to present this information.) For scientific or research papers, you will need to give the date, place, and audience to whom the paper was presented.

Use the following worksheet to help you gather the necessary information about your publications.

PUBLICATIONS

Title and Type (Note, Article, etc.) _____

Title of Publication (Journal, Book, etc.) _____

Publisher _____

Date Published _____

Title and Type (Note, Article, etc.) _____

Title of Publication (Journal, Book, etc.) _____

Publisher _____

Date Published _____

Title and Type (Note, Article, etc.) _____

Title of Publication (Journal, Book, etc.) _____

Publisher _____

Date Published _____

Professional Memberships

Another potential element in your resume is a section listing professional memberships. Use this section to describe your involvement in professional associations, unions, and similar organizations. It is to your advantage to list any professional memberships that pertain to the job you are seeking. Many employers see your membership as representative of your desire to stay up-to-date and connected in your field. Include the dates of your involvement and whether you took part in any special activities or held any offices within the organization. Use the following worksheet to organize your information.

PROFESSIONAL MEMBERSHIPS

Name of Organization _____

Office(s) Held_____

Activities _____

Dates _____

Name of Organization _____

Office(s) Held_____

Activities _____

Dates _____

Name of Organization _____

Office(s) Held_____

Activities _____

Dates _____

Name of Organization _____

Office(s) Held_____

Activities _____

Dates _____

Special Skills

The special skills section of your resume is the place to mention any special abilities you have that relate to the job you are seeking. You can use this element to present certain talents or experiences that are not necessarily a part of your education or work experience. Common examples include fluency in a foreign language, extensive travel abroad, or knowledge of a particular computer application. "Special skills" can encompass a wide range of talents, and this section can be used creatively. However, for each skill you list, you should be able to describe how it would be a direct asset in the type of work you're seeking because employers may ask just that in an interview. If you can't think of a way to do this, it may be extraneous information.

Personal Information

Some people include personal information on their resumes. This is generally not recommended, but you might wish to include it if you think that something in your personal life, such as a hobby or talent, has some bearing on the position you are seeking. This type of information is often referred to at the beginning of an interview, when it may be used as an icebreaker. Of course, personal information regarding your age, marital status, race, religion, or sexual orientation should never appear on your resume as personal information. It should be given only in the context of memberships and activities, and only when doing so would not expose you to discrimination.

References

References are not usually given on the resume itself, but a prospective employer needs to know that you have references who may be contacted if necessary. All you need to include is a single sentence at the end of the resume: "References are available upon request," or even simply, "References available." Have a reference list ready—your interviewer may ask to see it! Contact each person on the list ahead of time to see whether it is all right for you to use him or her as a reference. This way, the person has a chance to think about what to say *before* the call occurs. This helps ensure that you will obtain the best reference possible.

Chapter 2

Writing Your Resume

Now that you have gathered the information for each section of your resume, it's time to write it out in a way that will get the attention of the reviewer—hopefully, your future employer! The language you use in your resume will affect its success, so you must be careful and conscientious. Translate the facts you have gathered into the active, precise language of resume writing. You will be aiming for a resume that keeps the reader's interest and highlights your accomplishments in a concise and effective way.

Resume writing is unlike any other form of writing. Although your seventh-grade composition teacher would not approve, the rules of punctuation and sentence building are often completely ignored. Instead, you should try for a functional, direct writing style that focuses on the use of verbs and other words that imply action on your part. Writing with action words and strong verbs characterizes you to potential employers as an energetic, active person, someone who completes tasks and achieves results from his or her work. Resumes that do not make use of action words can sound passive and stale. These resumes are not effective and do not get the attention of any employer, no matter how qualified the applicant. Choose words that display your strengths and demonstrate your initiative. The following list of commonly used verbs will help you create a strong resume:

administered	assembled
advised	assumed responsibility
analyzed	billed
arranged	built

carried out	inspected
channeled	interviewed
collected	introduced
communicated	invented
compiled	maintained
completed	managed
conducted	met with
contacted	motivated
contracted	negotiated
coordinated	operated
counseled	orchestrated
created	ordered
cut	organized
designed	oversaw
determined	performed
developed	planned
directed	prepared
dispatched	presented
distributed	produced
documented	programmed
edited	published
established	purchased
expanded	recommended
functioned as	recorded
gathered	reduced
handled	referred
hired	represented
implemented	researched
improved	reviewed

saved	supervised
screened	taught
served as	tested
served on	trained
sold	typed
suggested	wrote

Let's look at two examples that differ only in their writing style. The first resume section is ineffective because it does not use action words to accent the applicant's work experiences.

WORK EXPERIENCE
Regional Sales Manager

Manager of sales representatives from seven states. Manager of twelve food chain accounts in the East. In charge of the sales force's planned selling toward specific goals. Supervisor and trainer of new sales representatives. Consulting for customers in the areas of inventory management and quality control.

Special Projects: Coordinator and sponsor of annual Food Industry Seminar.

Accomplishments: Monthly regional volume went up 25 percent during my tenure while, at the same time, a proper sales/cost ratio was maintained. Customer-company relations were improved.

In the following paragraph, we have rewritten the same section using action words. Notice how the tone has changed. It now sounds stronger and more active. This person accomplished goals and really *did* things.

WORK EXPERIENCE
Regional Sales Manager

Managed sales representatives from seven states. Oversaw twelve food chain accounts in the eastern United States. Directed the sales force in planned selling toward specific goals. Supervised and trained new sales representatives. Counseled customers in the areas of inventory management and quality control. Coordinated and sponsored the annual Food Industry Seminar. Increased monthly regional volume by 25 percent and helped to improve customer-company relations during my tenure.

One helpful way to construct the work experience section is to make use of your actual job descriptions—the written duties and expectations your employers have for a person in your current or former position. Job descriptions are rarely written in proper resume language, so you will have to rework them, but they do include much of the information necessary to create this section of your resume. If you have access to job descriptions for your former positions, you can use the details to construct an action-oriented paragraph. Often, your human resources department can provide a job description for your current position.

The following is an example of a typical human resources job description, followed by a rewritten version of the same description employing action words and specific details about the job. Again, pay attention to the style of writing instead of the content, as the details of your own experience will be unique.

WORK EXPERIENCE
Public Administrator I

Responsibilities: Coordinate and direct public services to meet the needs of the nation, state, or community. Analyze problems; work with special committees and public agencies; recommend solutions to governing bodies.

Aptitudes and Skills: Ability to relate to and communicate with people; solve complex problems through analysis; plan, organize, and implement policies and programs. Knowledge of political systems, financial management, personnel administration, program evaluation, and organizational theory.

WORK EXPERIENCE
Public Administrator I

Wrote pamphlets and conducted discussion groups to inform citizens of legislative processes and consumer issues. Organized and supervised 25 interviewers. Trained interviewers in effective communication skills.

After you have written out your resume, you are ready to begin the next important step: assembly and layout.

Chapter 3

Assembly and Layout

A t this point, you've gathered all the necessary information for your resume and rewritten it in language that will impress your potential employers. Your next step is to assemble the sections in a logical order and lay them out on the page neatly and attractively to achieve the desired effect: getting the interview.

Assembly

The order of the elements in a resume makes a difference in its overall effect. Clearly, you would not want to bury your name and address somewhere in the middle of the resume. Nor would you want to lead with a less important section, such as special skills. Put the elements in an order that stresses your most important accomplishments and the things that will be most appealing to your potential employer. For example, if you are new to the workforce, you will want the reviewer to read about your education and life skills before any part-time jobs you may have held for short durations. On the other hand, if you have been gainfully employed for several years and currently hold an important position in your company, you should list your work accomplishments ahead of your educational information, which has become less pertinent with time.

Certain things should always be included in your resume, but others are optional. The following list shows you which are which. You might want to use it as a checklist to be certain that you have included all of the necessary information.

Essential	**Optional**
Name	Cellular Phone Number
Address	Pager Number
Phone Number	E-Mail Address or Website Address
Work Experience	Voice Mail Number
Education	Job Objective
References Phrase	Honors
	Special Skills
	Publications
	Professional Memberships
	Activities
	Certificates and Licenses
	Personal Information
	Graphics
	Photograph

Your choice of optional sections depends on your own background and employment needs. Always use information that will put you in a favorable light—unless it's absolutely essential, avoid anything that will prompt the interviewer to ask questions about your weaknesses or something else that could be unflattering. Make sure your information is accurate and truthful. If your honors are impressive, include them in the resume. If your activities in school demonstrate talents that are necessary for the job you are seeking, allow space for a section on activities. If you are applying for a position that requires ornamental illustration, you may want to include border illustrations or graphics that demonstrate your talents in this area. If you are answering an advertisement for a job that requires certain physical traits, a photo of yourself might be appropriate. A person applying for a job as a computer programmer would *not* include a photo as part of his or her resume. Each resume is unique, just as each person is unique.

Types of Resumes

So far we have focused on the most common type of resume—the *reverse chronological* resume—in which your most recent job is listed first. This is the type of resume usually preferred by those who have to read a large number of resumes, and it is by far the most popular and widely circulated. However, this style of presentation may not be the most effective way to highlight *your* skills and accomplishments.

For example, if you are reentering the workforce after many years or are trying to change career fields, the *functional* resume may work best. This type of resume puts the focus on your achievements instead of the sequence of your work history. In the functional resume, your experience is presented through your general accomplishments and the skills you have developed in your working life.

A functional resume is assembled from the same information you gathered in Chapter 1. The main difference lies in how you organize the information. Essentially, the work experience section is divided in two, with your job duties and accomplishments constituting one section and your employers' names, cities, and states; your positions; and the dates employed making up the other. Place the first section near the top of your resume, just below your job objective (if used), and call it *Accomplishments* or *Achievements*. The second section, containing the bare essentials of your work history, should come after the accomplishments section and can be called *Employment History*, since it is a chronological overview of your former jobs.

The other sections of your resume remain the same. The work experience section is the only one affected in the functional format. By placing the section that focuses on your achievements at the beginning, you draw attention to these achievements. This puts less emphasis on where you worked and when, and more on what you did and what you are capable of doing.

If you are changing careers, the emphasis on skills and achievements is important. The identities of previous employers (who aren't part of your new career field) need to be downplayed. A functional resume can help accomplish this task. If you are reentering the workforce after a long absence, a functional resume is the obvious choice. And if you lack full-time work experience, you will need to draw attention away from this fact and put the focus on your skills and abilities. You may need to highlight your volunteer activities and part-time work. Education may also play a more important role in your resume.

The type of resume that is right for you will depend on your personal circumstances. It may be helpful to create both types and then compare them. Which one presents you in the best light? Examples of both types of resumes are included in this book. Use the sample resumes in Chapter 5 to help you decide on the content, presentation, and look of your own resume.

Resume or Curriculum Vitae?

A curriculum vitae (CV) is a longer, more detailed synopsis of your professional history, which generally runs three or more pages in length. It includes a summary of your educational and academic background as well as teaching and research experience, publications, presentations, awards, honors, affiliations, and other details. Because the purpose of the CV is different from that of the resume, many of the rules we've discussed thus far involving style and length do not apply.

A curriculum vitae is used primarily for admissions applications to graduate or professional schools, independent consulting in a variety of settings, proposals for fellowships or grants, or applications for positions in academia. As with a resume, you may need different versions of a CV for different types of positions. You should only send a CV when one is specifically requested by an employer or institution.

Like a resume, your CV should include your name, contact information, education, skills, and experience. In addition to the basics, a CV includes research and teaching experience, publications, grants and fellowships, professional associations and licenses, awards, and other information relevant to the position for which you are applying. You can follow the advice presented thus far to gather and organize your personal information.

Special Tips for Electronic Resumes

Because there are many details to consider in writing a resume that will be posted or transmitted on the Internet, or one that will be scanned into a computer when it is received, we suggest that you refer to the *Guide to Internet Job Searching*, by Frances Roehm and Margaret Dikel, as previously mentioned. However, here are some brief, general guidelines to follow if you expect your resume to be scanned into a computer.

- Use standard fonts in which none of the letters touch.

- Keep in mind that underlining, italics, and fancy scripts may not scan well.

- Use boldface and capitalization to set off elements. Again, make sure letters don't touch. Leave at least a quarter inch between lines of type.

- Keep information and elements at the left margin. Centering, columns, and even indenting may change when the resume is optically scanned.

- Do not use any lines, boxes, or graphics.

- Place the most important information at the top of the first page. If you use two pages, put "Page 1 of 2" at the bottom of the first page and put your name and "Page 2 of 2" at the top of the second page.

- List each telephone number on its own line in the header.

- Use multiple keywords or synonyms for what you do to make sure your qualifications will be picked up if a prospective employer is searching for them. Use nouns that are keywords for your profession.

- Be descriptive in your titles. For example, don't just use "assistant"; use "legal office assistant."

- Make sure the contrast between print and paper is good. Use a high-quality laser printer and white or very light colored 8½-by-11-inch paper.

- Mail a high-quality laser print or an excellent copy. Do not fold or use staples, as this might interfere with scanning. You may, however, use paper clips.

In addition to creating a resume that works well for scanning, you may want to have a resume that can be e-mailed to reviewers. Because you may not know what word processing application the recipient uses, the best format to use is ASCII text. (ASCII stands for "American Standard Code for Information Interchange.") It allows people with very different software platforms to exchange and understand information. (E-mail operates on this principle.) ASCII is a simple, text-only language, which means you can include only simple text. There can be no use of boldface, italics, or even paragraph indentations.

To create an ASCII resume, just use your normal word processing program; when finished, save it as a "text only" document. You will find this option under the "save" or "save as" command. Here is a list of things to *avoid* when crafting your electronic resume:

- Tabs. Use your space bar. Tabs will not work.

- Any special characters, such as mathematical symbols.

- Word wrap. Use hard returns (the return key) to make line breaks.

- Centering or other formatting. Align everything at the left margin.

- Bold or italic fonts. Everything will be converted to plain text when you save the file as a "text only" document.

Check carefully for any mistakes before you save the document as a text file. Spellcheck and proofread it several times; then ask someone with a keen eye to go over it again for you. Remember: the key is to keep it simple. Any attempt to make this resume pretty or decorative may result in a resume that is confusing and hard to read. After you have saved the document, you can cut and paste it into an e-mail or onto a website.

Layout for a Paper Resume

A great deal of care—and much more formatting—is necessary to achieve an attractive layout for your paper resume. There is no single appropriate layout that applies to every resume, but there are a few basic rules to follow in putting your resume on paper:

- Leave a comfortable margin on the sides, top, and bottom of the page (usually one to one and a half inches).

- Use appropriate spacing between the sections (two to three line spaces are usually adequate).

- Be consistent in the *type* of headings you use for different sections of your resume. For example, if you capitalize the heading EMPLOYMENT HISTORY, don't use initial capitals and underlining for a section of equal importance, such as Education.

- Do not use more than one font in your resume. Stay consistent by choosing a font that is fairly standard and easy to read, and don't change it for different sections. Beware of the tendency to try to make your resume original by choosing fancy type styles; your resume may end up looking unprofessional instead of creative. Unless you are in a very creative and artistic field, you should almost always stick with tried-and-true type styles like Times New Roman and Palatino, which are often used in business writing. In the area of resume styles, conservative is usually the best way to go.

CHRONOLOGICAL RESUME

Carter M. Winslow
555 Amsterdam Avenue
New York, NY 10024
carter.winslow@xxx.com
(212) 555-5727

Professional Objective
To secure a position as a social worker with an agency that will enable me to apply my eight years of counseling and administrative experience.

Employment History
Institute for Behavior Resources, Washington, DC
Director of Youth Group Program, March 2003 - present
- Program for neglected and abused children
- Responsible for staff of seven full-time caseworkers and six volunteers including screening and training of new staff members
- Program liaison with community and state agencies
- Prepared grant proposals, which accounted for 70 percent of program funding

Institute for Behavior Resources, Washington, DC
Youth Group Program Social Worker, October 1998 - March 2003
- Conducted psychosocial assessments and implemented appropriate counseling for neglected and abused children ages 7 - 12
- Conducted workshops for educators and day care personnel on identifying signs of neglect and abuse and the proper procedure for reporting cases of suspected abuse
- Served as consultant to State Child Welfare Department

George Washington University Medical Center, Washington, DC
Pediatric Ward Counselor, June 1997 - September 1998
- Led individual and group therapy sessions for children with physical injury–related trauma
- Counseled family members and designed and implemented support group for siblings of pediatric patients

Family and Child Services, Washington, DC
Social work intern, June 1996 - May 1997
- Collected statistical data on foster care placement of DC-area children for annual report presented to the Mayor's Council

Page 1 of 2

Employment History *(continued)*

Hope House, Washington, DC
Volunteer counselor, November 1994 - May 1996
Counseled children in safe house for battered women and their families

Education

George Washington University, Washington, DC
M.S.W., 1996

University of Maryland, College Park, MD
B.A., Psychology, 1994

References Available Upon Request

FUNCTIONAL RESUME

DAVID SWANSON
650 Clifton Avenue • Austin, TX 68143 • (612) 555-6915 • David.Swanson@xxx.com

SKILLS IN SUPERVISION
• Directed Head Start training program, evaluated teaching performances
• Recruited and trained Outward Bound volunteers
• Supervised work/study program, monitored student's job performance and employer satisfaction, recruited corporate participants

PROGRAM DESIGN AND ORGANIZATION
• Established course objectives, developed curriculum for Head Start
• Designed training program for Outward Bound volunteers
• Coordinated adult education program with government, corporate, and community agencies

COMMUNICATIONS
• Wrote federal grant proposal and lobbied for funding for Head Start
• Presented lectures to community and professional groups
• Developed training guides for Outward Bound volunteers

TEACHING
• Developed instructional aids and educational materials for adolescents and adults
• Increased motivation and program completion rates among at-risk students in adult education program

EMPLOYMENT
2000–Present
Director, Adult Education Program, High School District 84, Austin, TX

1997–2000
Director, Head Start, Atlanta, GA

1996–1997
Program Coordinator, Outward Bound, Atlanta, GA

EDUCATION
Georgia State University, M.Ed., Adult Education, 2000
Southern Methodist University, B.A., English, 1996

HONORS
Outstanding Teacher Award, 2000
Atlanta Community Service Medal, 1999

MEMBERSHIPS
American Society of Training and Development

References available upon request

- Always try to fit your resume on one page. If you are having trouble with this, you may be trying to say too much. Edit out any repetitive or unnecessary information, and shorten descriptions of earlier jobs where possible. Ask a friend you trust for feedback on what seems unnecessary or unimportant. For example, you may have included too many optional sections. Today, with the prevalence of the personal computer as a tool, there is no excuse for a poorly laid out resume. Experiment with variations until you are pleased with the result.

Remember that a resume is not an autobiography. Too much information will only get in the way. The more compact your resume, the easier it will be to review. If a person who is swamped with resumes looks at yours, catches the main points, and then calls you for an interview to fill in some of the details, your resume has already accomplished its task. A clear and concise resume makes for a happy reader and a good impression.

There are times when, despite extensive editing, the resume simply cannot fit on one page. In this case, the resume should be laid out on two pages in such a way that neither clarity nor appearance is compromised. Each page of a two-page resume should be marked clearly: the first should indicate "Page 1 of 2," and the second should include your name and the page number, for example, "Julia Ramirez—Page 2 of 2." The pages should then be paper-clipped together. You may use a smaller type size (in the same font as the body of your resume) for the page numbers. Place them at the bottom of page one and the top of page two. Again, spend the time now to experiment with the layout until you find one that looks good to you.

Always show your final layout to other people and ask them what they like or dislike about it, and what impresses them most when they read your resume. Make sure that their responses are the same as what you want to elicit from your prospective employer. If they aren't the same, you should continue to make changes until the necessary information is emphasized.

Proofreading

After you have finished typing the master copy of your resume and before you have it copied or printed, thoroughly check it for typing and spelling errors. Do not place all your trust in your computer's spellcheck function. Use an old editing trick and read the whole resume backward—start at the end and read it right to left and bottom to top. This can help you see the small errors or inconsistencies that are easy to overlook. Take time to do it right because a single error on a document this important can cause the reader to judge your attention to detail in a harsh light.

Have several people look at the finished resume just in case you've missed an error. Don't try to take a shortcut; not having an unbiased set of eyes examine your resume now could mean embarrassment later. Even experienced editors can easily overlook their own errors. Be thorough and conscientious with your proofreading so your first impression is a perfect one.

We have included the following rules of capitalization and punctuation to assist you in the final stage of creating your resume. Remember that resumes often require use of a shorthand style of writing that may include sentences without periods and other stylistic choices that break the standard rules of grammar. Be consistent in each section and throughout the whole resume with your choices.

RULES OF CAPITALIZATION

- Capitalize proper nouns, such as names of schools, colleges, and universities; names of companies; and brand names of products.

- Capitalize major words in the names and titles of books, tests, and articles that appear in the body of your resume.

- Capitalize words in major section headings of your resume.

- Do not capitalize words just because they seem important.

- When in doubt, consult a style manual such as *Words into Type* (Prentice Hall) or *The Chicago Manual of Style* (The University of Chicago Press). Your local library can help you locate these and other reference books. Many computer programs also have grammar help sections.

RULES OF PUNCTUATION

- Use commas to separate words in a series.

- Use a semicolon to separate series of words that already include commas within the series. (For an example, see the first rule of capitalization.)

- Use a semicolon to separate independent clauses that are not joined by a conjunction.

- Use a period to end a sentence.

- Use a colon to show that examples or details follow that will expand or amplify the preceding phrase.

- Avoid the use of dashes.

- Avoid the use of brackets.

- If you use any punctuation in an unusual way in your resume, be consistent in its use.

- Whenever you are uncertain, consult a style manual.

Putting Your Resume in Print

You will need to buy high-quality paper for your printer before you print your finished resume. Regular office paper is not good enough for resumes; the reviewer will probably think it looks flimsy and cheap. Go to an office supply store or copy shop and select a high-quality bond paper that will make a good first impression. Select colors like white, off-white, or possibly a light gray. In some industries, a pastel may be acceptable, but be sure the color and feel of the paper make a subtle, positive statement about you. Nothing in the choice of paper should be loud or unprofessional.

If your computer printer does not reproduce your resume properly and produces smudged or stuttered type, either ask to borrow a friend's or take your disk (or a clean original) to a printer or copy shop for high-quality copying. If you anticipate needing a large number of copies, taking your resume to a copy shop or a printer is probably the best choice.

Hold a sheet of your unprinted bond paper up to the light. If it has a watermark, you will want to point this out to the person helping you with copies; the printing should be done so that the reader can read the print and see the watermark the right way up. Check each copy for smudges or streaks. This is the time to be a perfectionist—the results of your careful preparation will be well worth it.

Chapter 4

The Cover Letter

Once your resume has been assembled, laid out, and printed to your satisfaction, the next and final step before distribution is to write your cover letter. Though there may be instances where you deliver your resume in person, you will usually send it through the mail or online. Resumes sent through the mail always need an accompanying letter that briefly introduces you and your resume. The purpose of the cover letter is to get a potential employer to read your resume, just as the purpose of the resume is to get that same potential employer to call you for an interview.

Like your resume, your cover letter should be clean, neat, and direct. A cover letter usually includes the following information:

1. Your name and address (unless it already appears on your personal letterhead) and your phone number(s); see item 7.

2. The date.

3. The name and address of the person and company to whom you are sending your resume.

4. The salutation ("Dear Mr." or "Dear Ms." followed by the person's last name, or "To Whom It May Concern" if you are answering a blind ad).

5. An opening paragraph explaining why you are writing (for example, in response to an ad, as a follow-up to a previous meeting, at the suggestion of someone you both know) and indicating that you are interested in whatever job is being offered.

6. One or more paragraphs that tell why you want to work for the company and what qualifications and experiences you can bring to the position. This is a good place to mention some detail about

that particular company that makes you want to work for them; this shows that you have done some research before applying.

7. A final paragraph that closes the letter and invites the reviewer to contact you for an interview. This can be a good place to tell the potential employer which method would be best to use when contacting you. Be sure to give the correct phone number and a good time to reach you, if that is important. You may mention here that your references are available upon request.

8. The closing ("Sincerely" or "Yours truly") followed by your signature in a dark ink, with your name typed under it.

Your cover letter should include all of this information and be no longer than one page in length. The language used should be polite, businesslike, and to the point. Don't attempt to tell your life story in the cover letter; a long and cluttered letter will serve only to annoy the reader. Remember that you need to mention only a few of your accomplishments and skills in the cover letter. The rest of your information is available in your resume. If your cover letter is a success, your resume will be read and all pertinent information reviewed by your prospective employer.

Producing the Cover Letter

Cover letters should always be individualized because they are always written to specific individuals and companies. Never use a form letter for your cover letter or copy it as you would a resume. Each cover letter should be unique, and as personal and lively as possible. (Of course, once you have written and rewritten your first cover letter until you are satisfied with it, you can certainly use similar wording in subsequent letters. You may want to save a template on your computer for future reference.) Keep a hard copy of each cover letter so you know exactly what you wrote in each one.

There are sample cover letters in Chapter 6. Use them as models or for ideas of how to assemble and lay out your own cover letters. Remember that every letter is unique and depends on the particular circumstances of the individual writing it and the job for which he or she is applying.

After you have written your cover letter, proofread it as thoroughly as you did your resume. Again, spelling or punctuation errors are a sure sign of carelessness, and you don't want that to be a part of your first impression on a prospective employer. This is no time to trust your spellcheck function. Even after going through a spelling and grammar check, your cover letter should be carefully proofread by at least one other person.

Print the cover letter on the same quality bond paper you used for your resume. Remember to sign it, using a good dark-ink pen. Handle the letter and resume carefully to avoid smudging or wrinkling, and mail them together in an appropriately sized envelope. Many stores sell matching envelopes to coordinate with your choice of bond paper.

Keep an accurate record of all resumes you send out and the results of each mailing. This record can be kept on your computer, in a calendar or notebook, or on file cards. Knowing when a resume is likely to have been received will keep you on track as you make follow-up phone calls.

About a week after mailing resumes and cover letters to potential employers, contact them by telephone. Confirm that your resume arrived and ask whether an interview might be possible. Be sure to record the name of the person you spoke to and any other information you gleaned from the conversation. It is wise to treat the person answering the phone with a great deal of respect; sometimes the assistant or receptionist has the ear of the person doing the hiring.

You should make a great impression with the strong, straightforward resume and personalized cover letter you have just created. We wish you every success in securing the career of your dreams!

Sample Resumes

This chapter contains dozens of sample resumes for people pursuing a wide variety of jobs and careers in social services.

There are many different styles of resumes in terms of graphic layout and presentation of information. These samples represent people with varying amounts of education and experience. Use them as models for your own resume. Choose one resume or borrow elements from several different resumes to help you construct your own.

MAY CHI XIONG

169 Schoolhouse Lane
Westbrook, CT 06498
Cell: (203) 555-9422
Email: m.xiong@xxx.com

EDUCATION

University of Connecticut, Stoors, CT.
M.Ed., 1999. Secondary education with English as a Second Language concentration. 3.8 G.P.A.

Wesleyan University, Middletown, CT.
B.A., 1994. English major, Spanish minor. Graduate of the Educational Studies Program.

WORK HISTORY

Middlesex County Board of Education, Middletown, CT.
May 2003 - present
- Coordinator of county ESL instruction.
- Revised ESL teacher training program.
- Initiated mandatory in-service programming for all county teachers regarding the instruction of non-English-speaking and bilingual students.
- Administer diagnostic tests and interpret data.
- Supervise six county ESL instructors.

Shoreline Educational Institute, Old Saybrook, CT.
July 2000 - 2003
- ESL instructor for non-English-speaking students including individual and group lessons.
- Consultant to Connecticut State Board of Education Special Education Department.

Guilford High School, Guilford, CT.
August 1996 - June 2000
- Planned and taught Spanish levels II and IV.
- Developed and supervised Spanish and Hmong curriculum for elementary school enrichment program.

WORK HISTORY (continued)

Morgan High School, Clinton, CT.
September 1994 - June 1996
• Secondary level Spanish teacher.
• Responsible for curriculum development and implementation.
• Introduced and advised school's Spanish club including international school exchanges.

CREDENTIALS
• Connecticut Board of Education Certified Teacher
• Association Member Connecticut ESL Instructors
• American Association of ESL Instructors

References and additional information provided on request.

MARIE LOUISE FORSYTHE

670 West Church Street
Seattle, WA 10602
m.forsythe@xxx.com
(313) 555-3945

OBJECTIVE PROFILE
Employment Counseling Position

- Six years' experience in public sector employment counseling
- Proven ability to prepare clients for the work force
- Excellent communication and organizational skills
- Effective liaison between federal agencies and local business community
- Innovative solutions to training and organizational challenges
- Diplomatic team player with strong leadership ability

EDUCATION

B.A., Psychology, Western Washington University, Bellingham, WA
M.Ed., Counseling, University of California, Los Angeles, CA
Certified Personnel Counselor (CPC), National Association of Personnel
Counselors

EXPERIENCE

Work Release Coordinator, 2003–Present
Women's Correctional Center, Seattle, WA
- Develop long-term occupational therapy program for female inmates focusing
  on skills, especially office skills and computer literacy.
- Contact business owners to arrange entry-level positions for inmates upon
  their release.
- Monitor employment progress of released inmates.
- Found corporate sponsor to donate computer equipment and software
  packages.
- Set up computer training classes in multiple applications.

Employment Counselor, 2000–2003
Employment Opportunity Commission, Tacoma, WA
- Conducted job-training class in basic clerical skills.
- Administered occupational testing.
- Provided instruction on resume preparation and employment interviewing
  skills.
- Arranged job interviews for clients with area businesses.

References furnished upon request.

SANDRA J. HOLLIS

24 Beech Hollow Lane
Gadsden, AL 35910
Home: (205) 555-6629
Cell: (205) 555-7905

EXPERIENCE

TOWN MANAGER, GADSDEN, AL. 2000–PRESENT
- Represent Gadsden in the transaction of its affairs with government agencies, community organizations, businesses, and town residents
- Supervise six department heads and provide for efficient delivery of financial, administrative, and other staff services
- Oversee the implementation and enforcement of ordinances and regulations
- Prepare and submit annual budget and manage town finances
- Make appropriate policy recommendations to Town Commissioners
- Coordinate municipal economic development policies
- Administer municipal elections and supervise voter registration
- Knowledgeable in infrastructure and development financing, zoning and subdivision practices, Community Development Block Grant regulations, property acquisitions, and procurement practices

ANNISTON BUSINESS CONSULTANTS, BIRMINGHAM, AL. 1998–2000
- Consultant to county offices, providing information and advice on financial matters
- Conducted personal finance seminars and consulted with individual clients
- Researched and wrote money management article for local newspaper

BUSINESS INSTRUCTOR, BIRMINGHAM COMMUNITY COLLEGE, BIRMINGHAM, AL.
1994–1998
- Taught four classes per semester
- As member of Business Education Committee, completed report containing recommendations for restructuring the college Business program
- Conducted mini-seminars on financial planning and investment for Seniors Program

HISTORY TEACHER, PIEDMONT MIDDLE SCHOOL, PIEDMONT, AL. 1988–1994
- Taught five history courses, including curriculum development, presentation, and evaluation of student achievement

EDUCATION

M.B.A., Alabama State University, 1993
B.A., History, Smith College, 1988

References available upon request

JANE FITZGERALD

208 Prince George Street • Annapolis, MD 21401
Jane.Fitzgerald@xxx.com • (301) 555-1799

EDUCATION

George Washington University, Washington, DC.
M.A. in Art Therapy, 2004.

Stockton State College, Pomona, NJ.
B.A. in Art with a Psychology minor, 1991.

EXPERIENCE

Center for Children, Inc., La Plata, MD.
January 2002 - Present.
• Individual and group therapist for victims of sexual abuse and their families.
• Initiated and supervised art therapy program for atonements with eating disorders.

Anne Arundel County Department of Social Services, Anne Arundel, MD.
November 1997 - December 2001.
• Individual and group therapist for sexually and physically abused children.
• Facilitator for staff enrichment group.

Charter Hospital, Charlottesville, VA.
March 1995 - September 1998.
• Provided art therapy to psychiatric patients in individual and group sessions.
• Served as treatment team member on the adult unit.
• Field supervisor for master-level interns.
• Staff enrichment coordinator.

Department of Human Services, Washington, DC.
November 1994 - March 1995.
• Assisted social worker with cases involving abused and neglected children.
• Responsibilities included counseling, field and family visits, and preparing materials for court hearings.

The Joseph P. Kennedy Institute, Washington, DC.
September 1992 - May 1994.
• Art therapist intern for developmentally disabled students ages 5 - 12.
• Worked with hyperactive children, Alzheimer's patients, and anorexics.

The Helmbold Education Center for the Mentally Handicapped, Ventnor, NJ.
January 1992 - June 1994.
• Psychology Intern.

EXPERIENCE (continued)

Department of Continuing Education, Stockton State College, Pomona, NJ.
June 1989 - May 1990.
• Adjunct Instructor of Art.

PRESENTATIONS

"Abuse Prevention for Children"
U.S. Naval Academy, MD, February 2004.

"A Special Blend: The Role of Creative Arts and Expressive Therapy"
Annual Meeting of the Associated Psychotherapists of Maryland, June 2002.

"Stress Management for Older Adults"
Senior Citizen Center, Anne Arundel, MD, December 2001.

PUBLICATIONS

"Art Therapy and the Abused Child"
American Journal of Child and Adolescent Psychiatric Nursing, August 2004.

"Art Therapy: An Effective Strategy in the Counseling of Alzheimer's Patients"
Arts in Psychotherapy journal, Fall 2001.

"Art Psychotherapy in the Treatment of the Chemically Dependent Patient"
Arts in Psychotherapy journal, Summer 2000.

AFFILIATIONS

The American Art Therapy Association: Credentialed Professional Member.

References Available Upon Request.

Carter M. Winslow

555 Amsterdam Avenue

New York, NY 10024

carter.winslow@xxx.com

(212) 555-5727

Professional Objective

To secure a position as a social worker with an agency that will enable me to apply my eight years of counseling and administrative experience.

Employment History

Institute for Behavior Resources, Washington, DC
Director of Youth Group Program, March 2003 - present
- Program for neglected and abused children
- Responsible for staff of seven full-time caseworkers and six volunteers including screening and training of new staff members
- Program liaison with community and state agencies
- Prepared grant proposals, which accounted for 70 percent of program funding

Institute for Behavior Resources, Washington, DC
Youth Group Program Social Worker, October 1998 - March 2003
- Conducted psychosocial assessments and implemented appropriate counseling for neglected and abused children ages 7 - 12
- Conducted workshops for educators and day care personnel on identifying signs of neglect and abuse and the proper procedure for reporting cases of suspected abuse
- Served as consultant to State Child Welfare Department

George Washington University Medical Center, Washington, DC
Pediatric Ward Counselor, June 1997 - September 1998
- Led individual and group therapy sessions for children with physical injury–related trauma
- Counseled family members and designed and implemented support group for siblings of pediatric patients

Family and Child Services, Washington, DC
Social work intern, June 1996 - May 1997
- Collected statistical data on foster care placement of DC-area children for annual report presented to the Mayor's Council

Employment History (continued)
Hope House, Washington, DC
Volunteer counselor, November 1994 - May 1996
• Counseled children in safe house for battered women and their families

Education
George Washington University, Washington, DC
M.S.W., 1996

University of Maryland, College Park, MD
B.A., Psychology, 1994

References Available Upon Request

Jonathan K. Sanders

6 Weybridge Place
Chapel Hill, NC 27514
jon.sanders@xxx.com
(910) 555-3469

Career Objective

To obtain a counseling position with a nonprofit organization that serves the needs of the homeless population.

Experience

2004 - present
Job Development Counselor, Job Find, Chapel Hill, NC

• Provided job counseling to homeless men in three area transitional housing programs.
• Increased community business participation in job placement program by 50 percent.
• Organized weekly employment workshops and quarterly job fairs.
• Increased revenue for job training 30 percent through community fundraising and 25 percent through federal grants.
• Wrote quarterly newsletter distributed to county businesses.
• Provided training seminars to shelter staffers throughout North Carolina regarding effective job counseling strategies.
• Developed a computer database system to track client activity, allowing the organization to cease using paper files.

2000 - 2004
Volunteer, Hewlett Men's Shelter, Chapel Hill, NC

• Responsible for overnight coverage of 12-bed facility two nights per week.
• Member of committee for volunteer recruitment.
• Chairperson fundraising committee.
• Provided information regarding social services programs.

Education

B.A., Business, 2004, University of North Carolina
Anticipate M.S.W., Spring 2007, Duke University

References Provided Upon Request.

Michael J. Hernandez

P.O. Box 406 • Sedona, AZ 86336
Mike.Hernandez@xxx.com • (602) 555-0926

Career Objective
A challenging position in speech therapy in which I have the opportunity to use my education and proven work experience to advance to an administrative position.

Work Experience
Assistant coordinator of speech therapy, October 2004–present
NovaCare, Flagstaff, AZ
◆ Assign cases to staff members, evaluate progress of interdisciplinary rehabilitation team, train new personnel, and serve as patient advocate.
◆ Administer individual treatment to patients with non–birth-related speech impairments.

Staff speech therapist, May 2000–July 2004
Flagstaff Health Department, Flagstaff, AZ
◆ Administered diagnostic tests, interpreted data, and developed appropriate treatments for clients ages 4 to 86.
◆ Supervised speech therapy interns.

Speech therapist, April 1998–May 2000
Ohio Public Schools, Columbus, OH
◆ Performed routine testing of school children.
◆ Provided individual and group therapy for first through sixth graders.
◆ Provided family support and education.
◆ Served as liaison between school and other community resources.

Speech therapy intern, January 1997–April 1998
Columbus Department of Social Services, Columbus, OH
◆ Assisted therapists in developing and implementing treatment.
◆ Oversaw diagnostic testing.

Substitute teacher, September 1995–December 1996
Columbus Public Schools, Columbus, OH

Education
1997   M.A., Speech Therapy, Ohio State University
1995   B.A., Education, Drew University

Certifications
Arizona State Licensed Speech Therapist
Certificate of Clinical Competence in Therapy

References Available Upon Request

Robert Martin
2108 Rusk Street
Beaumont, TX 77701
Bob.Martin@xxx.com
(409) 555-8740

Experience
Correctional Specialist, 2000 - present
Houston Correctional Center, Houston, TX
- Screen repeat juvenile offenders for potential placement in diversion programs.
- Perform assessments including conducting interviews with offenders, reviewing police reports, interpreting psychological data, and conferring with other state-appointed personnel.
- Determine appropriate diversion placement and monitor progress through visitations, interviews, and follow-up case reporting.

Live-in Counselor, 1995 - 1999
Long Lane Center, Liberty, TX
- Provided overnight supervision for 16 adolescent boys with history of juvenile delinquency.
- Provided individual and group alcohol and substance abuse counseling.
- Initiated after-school work placement program and peer support groups.
- Worked in conjunction with Department of Children's Services and Houston Correctional Department.

Coordinator of Volunteers, 1992 - 1999
Center Stage Youth Hotline, Houston, TX
- Supervised 22 volunteers for 24-hour youth hotline.
- Initiated after-school peer counseling program.

Police Officer, 1991 - 1993
Houston Police Department, Houston, TX
- Specialized in juvenile cases.
- Conducted seminars for educators and parents on issue of alcohol and substance abuse.
- Served as law enforcement liaison to Children's Court Appointed Advocacy Program.

Education
1995   B.A., Psychology, Texas State University
1991   Graduated, Houston Police Academy

References
Available Upon Request

Jennifer Sungentuk

4891 S. Inland Way • Spokane, WA 99204
j.sungentuk@xxx.com • (509) 555-2641

Career Objective

To obtain a position in which I can combine my teaching experience with my concern for the environment.

Work Experience

Field Instructor, 2004–present
Environmental Education Group, Kettle Falls, WA
- Provide environmental conservation education and appreciation to elementary school children
- Lead school groups on nature hikes in and around Coulee Dam National Recreation Area
- Prepare educational materials to supplement outdoor lessons
- Visit local schools and prepare resource materials for classroom teachers

Fourth and fifth grade science teacher, 1999–2004
Hanover Elementary School, Hanover, PA
- Performed all aspects of classroom management and instruction including lesson planning, evaluation, and reporting
- Initiated and supervised elementary science fair

Student teacher, 1998 school year
Frederick Elementary School, Abbotstown, PA
- Taught four elementary science classes

Education

1998, B.S. in Biology, Gettysburg College

Certifications

- Washington State Board of Education Elementary Certification
- Pennsylvania State Board of Education Master Educator, Elementary Certification

Memberships

- Friends of Earth
- Mt. Spokane Conservation Group Spokane Recycling Committee
- American Association of Environmental Educators

References Available Upon Request

▍Drew B. Hopkins ▍

14 Hayward Street
Yonkers, NY 10704
Home: (914) 555-0190
Cell: (917) 555-8172
Drew.Hopkins@xxx.com

Work Experience

Information Specialist, 2000–Present
Northeast Bankers Association, New York, NY
▌ Answer ready-reference and servicing-quality questions
▌ Complete in-depth manual research
▌ Researching and write monthly article for association magazine
▌ Utilize current Microsoft software proficiently

Research Librarian, 1997–1999
Queens Public Library, Queens, NY
▌ Supervised staff of five assistant research librarians
▌ Acquired research materials, including four new computers for public use
▌ Initiated co-operative program with area schools to introduce students to library resources

Head Librarian, 1995–1997
Assistant Librarian, 1992–1995
Amherst Public Library, Amherst, MA
▌ Managed all aspects of daily operation of 100,000-volume collection
▌ Facilitated library Senior Outreach Program and implemented Children's Storytime program

Library Aide, 1991–1992
University of Massachusetts, Boston, MA
▌ Assisted staff with routine shelving duties and student and faculty reference requests
▌ Automated cataloging of reserve materials
▌ Received Outstanding Student Aide Award

Education

1992   M.L.S., University of Massachusetts, Boston, MA
1990   B.A., Brandeis University, Waltham, WA

References

Available Upon Request

NICOLE M. FRANKLIN

8 Gaul Road, Apt. 23   Home: (516) 555-9042
North Setauket, NY 11733   Work: (516) 555-1640
                    Email: Nicole.Franklin@xxx.com

EXPERIENCE

Adult Education Family Literacy Educator, July 2004 - present
Setauket Board of Education, East Setauket, NY
- Teach in pilot program that combines GED tutoring with family and parenting skills training.
- Serve on teaching committee that designed program, developed instructional materials, and submitted proposal for state funding.
- Confer with Department of Social Services caseworkers to ensure program participants receive full range of services.
- Currently serve as a consultant to two area adult education programs.

Assistant/Clerk for the Even Start Family Literacy Program
August 2003 - June 2004
Setauket Board of Education, East Setauket, NY
- Tutored individuals, performed administrative tasks, initiated fundraising to provide computers for classroom instruction.
- Collected and computerized Even Start data for statistical reporting to State Board of Education.

Literacy Volunteer, December 2000 - July 2003
Middlemass Public Library, Setauket, NY
- Tutored adults in reading skills.
- Served on Volunteer Recruitment Committee.
- Trained new volunteers.

EDUCATION

B.A., Psychology, University of Connecticut, 2003

References furnished on request

Salvador Mendez
■ ■ ■

6413 North Sheridan Road, #2B • Chicago, Illinois 60626
(773) 555-8623 • Sal.Mendez@xxx.com

■ Education

10/00–Present
Doctoral Student, Institute for Clinical Social Work, Chicago, Illinois

9/96–5/98
Boston University, Boston, Massachusetts, Master of Social Work

9/9– 5/96
Bennet College, Millbrook, New York, Bachelor of Fine Arts

■ Experience

Social Worker
Crisis Intervention and Referral Service, Lutheran General Hospital, Park
Ridge, Illinois, Department of Psychiatry, 7/03–Present
■ Provide short-term and long-term psychotherapy to individuals,
  couples, and families
■ Conduct evaluations and disposition planning for psychiatric and
  emotionally traumatized patients and their families in the Emergency
  Room and Medical Clinic
■ Staff a 24-hour telephone hotline for suicide prevention, crisis
  counseling, and/or referrals
■ Participate in community outreach and training program

Social Work Intern
Massachusetts General Hospital, Boston, Massachusetts, 9/02–5/03
■ Served in an affective disorder inpatient unit
■ Provided family and individual psychotherapy
■ Performed as liaison between the family and the hospital
■ Performed family assessment and discharge planning
■ Coordinated team treatment

Part-time Counselor
Alternative Housing Systems, Belmont, Massachusetts, 7/02–4/03
■ Provided counseling, crisis intervention, and supervision of house
  management tasks in a halfway house for 10 adults with Borderline
  Personality Disorder

■ Experience (*continued*)

Social Work Intern
Cunningham House Mental Health Center, Boston, Massachusetts,
9/01–5/02
Cunningham House is a mental health clinic within a multi-service
community agency.

■ Provided psychotherapy to individuals and groups, adults and
children, with problems such as personality disorders, behavioral
disturbances, anxiety, depression, and substance/alcohol abuse

Literacy Volunteer
Millbrook Public Library, Millbrook, New York, 10/00–8/01

■ Taught multilevel reading classes to primarily Hispanic and Eastern
European immigrants in both classroom and industrial settings

References Available Upon Request

GREG SIMON

947 W. Harwood Road
Lawrenceburg, IN 47025
g.simon@xxx.com
(812) 555-5680

WORK EXPERIENCE

2004 - Present
Lawrenceburg Police Department Patrolman, Field Operations Division

2003
Lawrenceburg High School, High School Liaison Officer, Investigation Division
Special Patrol, Juvenile and Criminal Investigations

1997 - 2003
Indianapolis Police Department Staff Aide, Criminalistics Division

EDUCATION

1997
B.S. in Law Enforcement Administration. Indiana Central University, Indianapolis, IN Comprehensive Major Program combining Political Science, Sociology, and Psychology

Police Training Institute. South Bend, IN
Basic 10-week training; graduated #2 in class

PROFESSIONAL CERTIFICATIONS

- Special Weapons and Tactics
- Arson
- Investigation
- Firearms Instructor
- Narcotics Investigation
- Evidence Technician
- Alcohol Testing

PROFESSIONAL MEMBERSHIPS

- Fraternal Order of Police
- Indiana Juvenile Officers

REFERENCES

Available Upon Request

MICHELLE JUNG

28 Elm Street

Brockton, MA 02403

Michelle.Jung@xxx.com

(508) 555-6843

OBJECTIVE

To empower clients to improve their lives through wise personal and career decisions

EXPERIENCE

Owner, Jung Associates, Inc. (1997 - present)
Achievements:
• Provided successful private career counseling for a wide variety of corporate and individual clients
• Developed and presented seminars for women returning to the workforce
• Conducted retirement-planning workshops for members of YMCA and local church organizations
• Served as career consultant to Mount Holyoke College and assisted in organization and development of internship program at the college

Director, Mount Holyoke Career Center (1993 - 1997)
Achievements:
• Provided career counseling and planning services to students
• Organized and directed annual career fair
• Conducted resume workshop for graduating seniors

EDUCATION

M.A., Guidance and Counseling, California State University-Sacramento, 1995
B.A., Psychology, University of New Mexico, 1993

PROFESSIONAL MEMBERSHIPS

• National Association of Counseling and Development
• Career Education Association of New England
• American Psychological Association

PUBLICATIONS

"Job Search Strategies for Graduating Seniors," *Career Bulletin*, October 2003
"Part-time Solutions for Working Mothers," *Career Express*, January 2003

References Provided Upon Request

allan a. mcfarlan

5448 W. Fournier Road
Westerly, RI 02891
Home: 401-555-4191
Cell: 401-555-0892
Email: Allan.McFarlan@xxx.com

objective

To obtain a library science position that utilizes my skills in developing and maintaining a large collection of texts and assisting patrons or students with research projects

work experience

2002–Present
Head Librarian, Providence College
• Supervise acquisition decisions for college library
• Direct staff of five librarians
• Develop annual budget recommendations
• Oversaw updating and automation of cataloguing system
• Train new employees on computerized catalog

1991–2002
Reference Librarian, Westerly Public Library
• Cataloged new materials for and maintained reference collection
• Organized and directed after-hours reference service
• Assisted patrons to find required materials
• Requested materials from and coordinated with other city libraries

education

M.A., Library Science, Rosary College, 1996
B.A., English, Northern Illinois University, 1991

References Available

Mary A. Griffin

102 N. Edgewater Court ❱ Easton, PA 18042 ❱ M.Griffin@xxx.com
(215) 555-8815

Professional Experience

Director, Easton Community Senior Center, Easton, PA, 1995–present

Teacher, Shelton School, Easton, PA, 1990–1995
❱ Taught third and fourth grade classes

Public Relations

❱ Developed membership program through increasing services and incentives
❱ Designed and developed a monthly newsletter using desktop publishing systems
❱ Arranged press conferences and prepared press kits
❱ Participated in community events and gave presentations at civic functions

Financial Management

❱ Prepared annual reports and monthly statements
❱ Developed a computerized bookkeeping system
❱ Created a volunteer workforce of more than 40 members
❱ Wrote grant proposals and implemented fund-raising activities to provide more than 90 percent of the budget
❱ Increased budget by 80 percent during tenure

Program Development

❱ Created and implemented 50 activities including healthcare, educational, and legal services
❱ Organized recreational programs, classes, trips, and special events

Awards

Governor's Hometown Award, 2004

Education

Bachelor of Science/Education, University of Pittsburgh, 1990

Certificate of Business Administration, Law Program for Community Developers, Point Park College, 1994

Skills

❱ Microsoft Office Suite including database management, desktop publishing, spreadsheets, and presentations
❱ Managing budgets and finances
❱ Strong organizational, management, marketing, and sales skills

References Available on Request

TERRELL BANKSTON, L.C.S.W.

1026 River Road
Columbia, MO 65201
T.Bankston@xxx.com
(314) 555-1678

PROFESSIONAL OBJECTIVE

A position as a psychotherapist in a clinical setting requiring proven skills in assessment; treatment, planning, and delivery; individual, couple, family, and group treatment.

QUALIFICATIONS

- Four years' experience in a mental health hospital psychiatric unit, community mental health center, drug dependence treatment center, and hospital outpatient unit.
- Experienced in program planning and delivery and working with the elderly.
- Excellent communication, negotiation, team-building, and problem-solving skills.

EXPERIENCE

Crisis Therapist, Boone Hospital Center, Columbia, MO, 2004–present.

- Staff a 24-hour telephone hotline for suicide prevention, crisis counseling, and/or referral.
- Provide brief intensive psychotherapy to individuals, couples, and families who need immediate treatment for a variety of emotional crises such as a death or divorce, and victims of accidents and assaults.
- Treat patients for symptoms such as anxiety, panic disorder, depression, post-traumatic stress disorder, and adjustment reactions to marital and family problems.
- Conduct emergency room evaluations of persons who present with symptoms of chronic mental illness or any kind of emotional trauma such as rape or domestic violence.

Addiction Therapist, Holy Cross Hospital, Columbia, MO, 2001–2004.

- Conducted assessments for alcohol and/or drug addiction.
- Organized comprehensive treatment plans.
- Developed educational programs and materials.
- Provided therapy for individuals and couples recovering from alcohol and/or drug addiction or the effects of the addiction of other family members.

EXPERIENCE (CONTINUED)

Intern Therapist, Wetzel Center/University of Missouri, Columbia, MO, 2000–2001.
- Provided therapy to individuals, couples, and families with a variety of presenting problems including addiction, incest, and narcissistic personality disorders.
- Participated in intensive intervention program that served families in crisis.
- Worked in innovative short-term family program that emphasized immediate solutions.
- Provided appropriate referrals to meet individual needs of clients and client systems.

Intern Therapist, St. Luke Medical Center, Columbia, MO, 1999–2000.
- Provided therapy for chronically mentally ill patients and their families.
- Served as support for patients in hospital.
- Participated in interdisciplinary treatment program.
- Collaborated with nurses, social workers, and psychiatrists.

EDUCATION

Master of Social Work from University of Missouri, Columbia, MO, 1999.
Bachelor of Arts from Kenyon College, Gambier, OH, 1997.

References furnished upon request.

VELIO A. PANSERA

8415 Oketo Avenue • Niles, IL 60714 • V.Pansera@xxx.com • (847) 555-7102

CAREER OBJECTIVE

To obtain a position as a school psychologist

EDUCATION

National-Louis University, Evanston, IL
Degree: Educational Specialist in School Psychology, 2005

Loyola University, Chicago, IL
Degree: Master of Arts, Clinical Psychology, 2003

Illinois State University, Normal, IL
Degree: Bachelor of Arts, 2000
Sociology and Psychology

CERTIFICATION

Type 73 Illinois School Board of Education

WORK EXPERIENCE

8/04 - present
Glenview North High School, Glenview, IL
School Psychology Intern
• Administer and interpret psychological and educational diagnostic tests
• Lead group counseling sessions
• Conduct individual counseling sessions
• Teach social skills classes to special education students
• Coach Junior Girls Softball

8/03 - 8/04
Martin Academy, Niles, IL
Therapist and Teacher Assistant
• Worked as a team member to develop appropriate levels of academic and behavioral assistance for students ages 10 to 19
• Participated in crisis intervention team
• Directed group therapy sessions

WORK EXPERIENCE (continued)

6/03 - 8/03
Tauber Mental Health Center, Mundelein, IL
Psychology Intern
- Administered psychological tests
- Counseled chemically dependent adolescents
- Conducted individual and group therapy

Summer 2002
Niles Park District, Niles, IL
Volleyball Day Camp Supervisor
- Taught basic fundamentals of volleyball to boys and girls ages 9 to 17
- Explained team strategies and instructed students on how to execute strategies

Fall 2000
St. Luke's Academy, Des Plaines, IL
Intern and Family Educator
- Served as a family educator for a home housing young women ages 6 to 17
- Worked with physically, emotionally, mentally, and sexually abused young women
- Assisted in the application of a behavior modification system

Fall 1999
Illinois State University, Normal, IL
Student Volunteer, Head Start Program
- Assisted in classroom activities
- Worked with children ages 3 to 5

MEMBERSHIPS
American Psychological Association
Illinois School Psychologists Association

References Available

CHRISTINA RIVERA

607 Ramsey Drive
Arlington, Virginia 22209
C.Rivera@xxx.com
(703) 555-2821

CAREER OBJECTIVE

Seeking a full-time teaching position in an urban public school that enables me to combine my primary-level teaching experience with my newly acquired Special Education degree.

EDUCATION

- University of Virginia, Charlottesville: M.Ed., Learning Disabilities/Behavior Disorders, December 2005
- Indiana University, Bloomington, Indiana: B.S., Elementary Education, May 2003

CERTIFICATION

- Virginia Special Education, Learning Disabilities and Social/Emotional Disorders, December 2005
- Virginia Standard Teaching License, Grades K–9, June 2003

PROFESSIONAL EXPERIENCE

- Kindergarten teacher, St. Margaret Mary School, Arlington, Virginia, 2004–present
- Kindergarten teacher, St. Francis School, Richmond, Virginia, 2003–2004
- Student teacher, St. Francis School, Grade 4, January–May 2003

RELATED EXPERIENCE

- Special Education Tutor, Learning Center, Richmond, Virginia, 2005
- Camp Counselor, Camp Deerpath, Baltimore, Maryland, 2003
- Volunteer, Junior High Girls Club leader, Richmond Community Center, summers 1999–2002

ACTIVITIES AND HONORS

- Curriculum Committee, St. Margaret Mary School, 2005
- Science Fair Committee, St. Francis School, 2004
- Talent Show Committee, St. Francis School, 2004
- Chair, Philanthropy Committee, Delta Delta Delta Sorority
- Chair, Alumna Relations, Delta Delta Delta Sorority
- Outstanding College Senior Award, Delta Delta Delta Sorority

PROFESSIONAL MEMBERSHIPS

- Orton Dyslexia Society
- Indiana University School of Education Professional Organization, Program Committee
- Indiana University Student Foundation, Special Projects Committee

REFERENCES

Mary Price, Principal, St. Margaret Mary School, Arlington, Virginia

John Cook, Vice-Principal, St. Margaret Mary School, Arlington, Virginia

Barb Fenwick, Supervisor, Learning Center, Richmond, Virginia

Michael Hernandez, Former Principal, St. Francis School, Richmond, Virginia

THOMAS LUTHRA

33 Humphrey Street, Apt. 2B • Washington, DC 20059
Cell: (301) 555-0987 • Business: (301) 555-5347
Email: Tom.Luthra@xxx.com

BACKGROUND

Expertise in individual and group guidance and counseling of faculty, students, and administrators in career, personal, and academic concerns; international business experience; efficient and effective management skills; diverse public speaking, consulting, and instructional experience in America and abroad.

ADMINISTRATION/COORDINATION

Director, Career Planning Center, Howard University, Washington, DC, 2002–Present

- Administer career development program for liberal arts students, faculty, staff, representatives of employing institutions, and representatives of graduate and professional schools.
- Supervise staff of nineteen: four assistant directors, three secretaries, and twelve students.
- Plan, implement, and coordinate seminars, workshops, counseling and referral services.
- Disseminate career information to appropriate constituencies.
- Provide special counseling and advice for pre-law and science students interested in business, public service, and international affairs.

Ex-officio member, Graduate Fellowship Committee, Howard University, 1991–2005

- Advise and counsel students applying for such fellowships, scholarships, and grants as Mellon, Fulbright, Rhodes, Marshall, Watson, Churchill, and St. Andrews; serve as campus liaison with above sponsors; prepare credentials of applicants for review by committee.

Assistant Dean for Supportive Services, Howard University, 1997–2001

- Supervised professional staff of seven including Assistant Director of University Scholars Program, Director of Math Clinic, Director of Writing Program, and Director of the Higher Educational Opportunity Program, with Washington, DC, Department of Education.
- Managed budget of $900,000.

Chair, Search Committee for Dean of Students, Howard University, 2001

Chair, Search Committee for College President, Howard University, 2000

Chair, Search Committee for Director of Writing Program, Howard University, 1998

Associate Dean of Students, Missouri Southern State College, Joplin, MO, 1989–1997
- Counseled and guided students regarding personal, educational, and career concerns.
- Served on tripartite committees such as Judicial Board, Curriculum Committee, and Campus Council.

Director, Career Planning, Missouri Southern State College, 1986–1989
- Administered career development program for liberal arts students, faculty, administrators, and representatives of prospective employers.
- Designed workshops and seminars, including Life Planning, Decision Making, New Directions (career exploration).

Director/Consultant, Tehran English Language Institute, Tehran, Iran, 1984–1986
- Administered teaching programs in conjunction with Iranian Ministries of Education and Higher Education.

CONSULTATION

Consultant/Counselor, Thomas J. Watson Foundation
Northeastern University, Boston, MA, Summer 2000
- Counseled sixty returning Watson Fellows regarding fellowship year.

Head, Evaluation Team, Career Development Office
Stanford University, Stanford, CA, 1996

EDUCATION

Invited Participant, International Seminar on Career Planning
Oxford University, Oxford, England, Fall 2004

Participant, Institute for Educational Guidance
Stanford University, Stanford, CA, Summer 1999

M.A., Teaching English as a Foreign Language, Teachers College
Columbia University, New York, NY, 1984

Course Work, Middle Eastern Culture, History, and Religion
University of Tehran, Tehran, Iran, 1978–1979

EDUCATION (continued)
M.Ed., Religious Education and Counseling
University of Southern Maine, Portland, ME, 1978

B.B.A., Economics and Business Administration
Westminster College, New Wilmington, PA, 1972

PUBLICATIONS
"Life's Work," Chicago, IL: The Career Press, 2005.

"The ESL Conversation Class," *English Teaching Journal*, vol. V (March–April, 1996), no. 1, 19–20. Republished in *English Teaching Journal*, Special Issue, vol. XIV, 2003.

"Career Counseling and the Student of Color," in *New Directions in the Millennium: Career Development*, edited by Casey Wendell. New York: University Holdings Press, 2000.

AWARDS
Silver Medal Award for alumni service to Howard University, Council for Advancement and Support of Education, 2001

Faculty Development Award, Howard University, 1999

MEMBERSHIPS
College Personnel Officers
National Association of Pre-Law Advisors

References Available Upon Request.

Sandra McQuiston

200 E. Third Avenue
St. Paul, MN 55415
sandy.mcquiston@xxx.com
(651) 555-4732

Experience

Director, 2003 to Present
Campus Counseling Center, College of St. Catherine, St. Paul, MN
• Direct college counseling service providing educational, vocational, and
  personal counseling to students, faculty, and staff.
• Supervise staff of three: counselor, administrative assistant, and student intern.
• Conduct extensive outreach program in campus community.
• Present workshops on topics such as stress management and assertiveness.

Owner, 1999 to 2002
Private Counseling Practice, Minneapolis, MN
• Provided personal, educational, and career counseling to individuals, groups,
  and corporations.
• Assisted private corporations with outplacement programs.
• Consultant to Uptown Community Health Center, helping design and
  implement crisis intervention hotline.

Counselor, 1995 to 1999
St. Paul Public School System, St. Paul, MN
• Administered and interpreted vocational interest inventories.
• Provided career information and counseling to public school students.

Education

St. Thomas University, M.Ed., Counseling, 1995
Knox College, B.A., English, 1993

Professional Memberships

National Association of Collegiate Career Counselors
American Society for Vocational Counseling

References Available

✳ KIMBERLY LEE ✳

918 W. Vine Street • Paw Paw, MI 49079
(616) 555-8645 • kim.lee@xxx.com

✳ OBJECTIVE

To pursue a career in a criminal or social service setting working for, and with, minors.

✳ EDUCATION

M.S.W.
Concentration: Clinical Social Work
Grand Valley State University, Grand Rapids, MI
Expected June 2007

B.A.
Major in Criminal Justice; Minor in Social Work
Grand Valley State University, Grand Rapids, MI
December 2003

A.A.
Major, Liberal Studies
Grand Rapids Community College, Grand Rapids, MI
December 2001

✳ PROFESSIONAL EXPERIENCE

Kent County Services, Caseworker III, Grand Rapids, MI
November 2005 - Present
Conduct investigations and submit intensive social studies involving private adoption placements and contested adoptions. In addition, investigate, by court order, the social conditions and residences of children whose parents are involved in divorce, paternity, and probate-related custody and visitation issues. Serve as an expert witness when subpoenaed.

✳ PROFESSIONAL INTERNSHIPS

Board of Education, Caledonia Public School System, Caledonia, MI
September 2003 - June 2004
Provided individual, family, and group treatment to children and their families. Participated in child placements with a multi-disciplinary staff.

Page 1 of 2

❋ PROFESSIONAL INTERNSHIPS (CONTINUED)

Office of the Public, Grand Rapids, MI
January 2004 - September 2004
Interviewed children and adolescents to assess and document factual
background of abuse and/or neglect prior to court hearings.
Assessment concluded with in-home evaluation.

Circuit Court of Kent County/Juvenile Division, Grand Rapids, MI
Spring 2003
Assisted probation officers with court duties on cases related to
minor respondents, participated in field surveillance and home visits
of minors, and completed and filed monthly and quarterly reports of
minors' progress.

❋ PROFESSIONAL MEMBERSHIPS

Michigan Social Work Council
National Association of Social Workers

References available on request.

DAVID SWANSON
650 Clifton Avenue • Austin, TX 68143 • (612) 555-6915 • David.Swanson@xxx.com

SKILLS IN SUPERVISION
• Directed Head Start training program, evaluated teaching performances
• Recruited and trained Outward Bound volunteers
• Supervised work/study program, monitored students' job performance and employer satisfaction, recruited corporate participants

PROGRAM DESIGN AND ORGANIZATION
• Established course objectives, developed curriculum for Head Start
• Designed training program for Outward Bound volunteers
• Coordinated adult education program with government, corporate, and community agencies

COMMUNICATIONS
• Wrote federal grant proposal and lobbied for funding for Head Start
• Presented lectures to community and professional groups
• Developed training guides for Outward Bound volunteers

TEACHING
• Developed instructional aids and educational materials for adolescents and adults
• Increased motivation and program completion rates among at-risk students in adult education program

EMPLOYMENT
2000–Present
Director, Adult Education Program, High School District 84, Austin, TX

1997–2000
Director, Head Start, Atlanta, GA

1996–1997
Program Coordinator, Outward Bound, Atlanta, GA

EDUCATION
Georgia State University, M.Ed., Adult Education, 2000
Southern Methodist University, B.A., English, 1996

HONORS
Outstanding Teacher Award, 2000
Atlanta Community Service Medal, 1999

MEMBERSHIP
American Society of Training and Development

References available upon request

JUAN MARTINEZ

2453 Cambridge Road
Kansas City, MO 64108
Cell Phone: (681) 555-8976
Email: juan.martinez@xxx.com

JOB OBJECTIVE
A library science position that will utilize my management and materials
acquisitions skills

CAPABILITIES
• Review purchasing materials and suggest acquisitions
• Develop quarterly budgets
• Act as community liaison
• Create publicity materials
• Study and report on the condition of special collections
• Handle reference calls and requests
• Assist patrons with new computer reference system

ACHIEVEMENTS
• Developed community outreach program that increased library use
• Developed successful budget proposals
• Trained and monitored volunteers
• Supervised staff of six
• Updated and expanded reference library
• Developed specialized science collection

EMPLOYMENT
2003 - Present
Librarian, Kansas City Public Libraries, Kansas City, MO

2000 - 2003
Head Librarian, Wright High School, Kansas City, MO

EDUCATION
M.L.S., Rosary College, River Forest, IL, Library Science, 2000

B.S., State University of New York–Buffalo, Biology, 1998

REFERENCES AVAILABLE

MILTON R. ROSENBURG

650 Second Street • Portland, OR 97204

M.Rosenburg@xxx.com • (503) 555-6418

EXPERIENCE

Counselor, Portland Mental Health Center, Portland, OR, 2002–Present
• Counsel youth and adult population; suggest treatment options for drug and
  alcohol dependence:
• Refer patients to other private and community organizations for medical and
  social support.
• Maintain accurate, detailed records of weekly counseling sessions.
• Organize and lead ongoing addiction support groups.

Coordinator, Seattle Community Recreation Center, Seattle, WA, 1999–2002
• Planned and created community recreation center; supervised activities for
  local youth.
• Wrote funding proposal for town council.
• Recruited volunteer staff and members.
• Purchased all supplies online.
• Designed publicity materials using Publisher.

Student Activities Director, Pacific Lutheran U., Tacoma, WA, 1995–1999
• Planned and directed student activities including live entertainment and
  special events.
• Supervised student activities committee.
• Booked and publicized events.
• Supervised staff of four.
• Negotiated contracts with vendors.

EDUCATION

University of Oregon, 1994
B.S., Leisure and Recreation

SKILLS

• Proficient in using Microsoft programs including Excel, Word, PowerPoint,
  and Publisher.
• Fluent in Spanish and French.

PROFESSIONAL ASSOCIATIONS

Portland Youth Council
National Recreation Alliance

REFERENCES AVAILABLE ON REQUEST.

Shira Brown

614 North White Street
Arlington Heights, IL 60004
Shira.Brown@xxx.com
(708) 555-8604

Education

B.S./R.N., Northern Illinois University, DeKalb, IL
Specializing in community health and pediatric issues
Type 73 special service certificate

Employment

January 2003 to Present
Instructor of Family Living at Glenwood High School, Young Adult Education
Program
- Teach four periods a day to 9–12 grades.
- Educate on all aspects of community health from sexually transmitted diseases to childbirth and rearing.
- Work with community partners to assure the most relevant issues and public speakers as possible.

October 1998 to January 2003
Parental Leave

August 1996 to October 1998
School Nurse, Wheaton Elementary School, District 63
- Responsible for participation in child study team, development of health curriculum, vision and hearing screenings, and first aid.
- Discussed issues with parents and referred them when necessary.
- Assisted children with daily medicine doses.
- Monitored for infectious symptoms and outbreaks.

July 1993 to August 1996
Public Health Nurse, DuPage County Health Department
- Responsible for school nursing and organization of, and participation in, well-child clinic.
- Led the home care of elderly and ill.
- Supervised home health aides.
- Coordinated with the mental health department on cooperative programs.

References Available on Request.

■ ■ ■ ANN OLIVERA ■ ■ ■
664 E. Ivy Drive
Nashville, TN 37212
615/555-4573

■ ■ ■ EXPERIENCE

Supervisor, Intake Unit, Greater Nashville Social Services, 2002 - Present
- ■ Supervise four workers assigned to interview and assess parties involved in private adoption proceedings.
- ■ Log, track, and assign cases.
- ■ Witness consents by biological parents for the adoption of their children.
- ■ Record fees for adoption studies and subpoenas.
- ■ Review and plan strategies (with collaboration of coworkers) on problem cases.

Caseworker/Child Custody Worker, Greater Nashville Social Services,
1996 - 2002
- ■ Handled approximately 1,000 child custody mediation cases and more than 50 child custody and adoption investigations.
- ■ Experience in Municipal Division (in parentage cases) and in Domestic Relations Division.
- ■ Served as mediator and expert witness.
- ■ Handled emergency cases.

Part-Time Counselor/Office Manager, Office of Veterans Affairs, Tennessee
State University, 1994 - 1996
- ■ Advised student veterans on many issues and supervised other employees in these capacities.
- ■ Helped to write and edit proposal for program funding and to determine and allocate budget.

■ ■ ■ EDUCATION

Master's Degree in Social Work, Hillcrest School of Social Work, 2001
- ■ Concentration in mental health.

Clinical internship at Nashville Family Services and Community Mental Health Center, Child and Adolescent Unit, 2001 - 2002
- ■ Acted as therapist, making provisional diagnoses and consulting with staff.

■ ■ ■ EDUCATION *(continued)*

Clinical internship at Providence Crisis Center, 2000 - 2001
■ Provided services to victims and perpetrators of domestic violence.
■ Served as therapist and intake evaluator.

Master of Arts in Teaching (with honors), Temple University, 1994
■ Thesis/Research Project: Analysis of Gender Differences in the Syntax of Student Writing.

Bachelor of Arts, City College of New York, 1991
■ Magna Cum Laude.

■ ■ ■ PUBLICATIONS

Article, "Decision-Making Alternatives in Child Custody Mediation," in *Family Counseling Quarterly*, vol. 7, no. 3, Spring 2004.

Work in progress: "Security Issues at Women's Shelters: Implications for Domestic Violence Treatment."

■ ■ ■ REFERENCES

Lynne Schickel, Former Supervisor, Providence Crisis Center, now a marriage and family counseling mediator in private practice: (615) 555-8965.

John Gilroy, Director, Nashville Family Services and Community Mental Health Center: (615) 555-8756.

James Kortis, Supervisor, Greater Nashville Social Services: (615) 555-4321.

■ ■ ■ PROFESSIONAL MEMBERSHIPS AND LICENSURES

■ State of Tennessee Licensed Social Worker
■ Member, National Association of Social Workers
■ Member, American Alliance for the Prevention of Domestic Violence

ALEC RAJIK

25 Lake Street
Milwaukee, WI 53404
Alec.Rajik@xxx.com
414-908-5623

OBJECTIVE

A position in health policy administration that makes use of my expertise as a disease control specialist

SKILLS

- Ability to conduct investigations and develop and implement disease control
- Knowledge of public health administration
- Health care crisis management skills
- Disciplined work habits
- Strong organizational skills
- Ability to meet tight deadlines and function smoothly under pressure

EXPERIENCE

- Extensive background in public health
- Experience in Milwaukee Department of Health with Dr. Langley
- Investigated lethal outbreak of cryptosporidium in Milwaukee water system
- Published paper on blood shortage in *National Journal of Health*
- Claims adjustor for American Insurance Company

EMPLOYMENT

Medical Technologist, Milwaukee Community Blood Bank
2004–Present

Disease Control Consultant, Madison Department of Health
2000–2004

Claims Adjustor, American Insurance Company
1997–2000

EDUCATION

M.A. in Public Health, University of Wisconsin, Madison, 2000
B.A. in Communications, University of Wisconsin, Madison, 1997

REFERENCES AVAILABLE UPON REQUEST

Carmen Fajardo

944 Grace Street • Modesto, CA 93201 • 916-555-5642 • carmen.fajardo@xxx.com

Professional Background

Diverse professional background with experience in the following: compilation and statistical analysis of medical and scientific data, abstracting and indexing of technical material, medical library science, clinical laboratory work.

Skills

Leadership ability, strong management skills, public speaking experience, excellent organizational skills.

Employment History

Hughes Pharmaceutical Supply, Modesto, CA
Position: Medical Reference Librarian, 2003 - Present
• Abstract and index articles from medical reference material.
• Compile research materials for sales, legal, and marketing professionals.

Warren County Hospital, Sacramento, CA
Position: Medical Records Supervisor, 2001 - 2003
• Modernized online medical records system.
• Supervised medical records clerks.
• Created standardized records procedure and conducted in-service seminars on use of new system for all affected departments.

Davis General Hospital, Davis, CA
Position: Clinical Laboratory Technician, 1998 - 2001
• Performed clinical testing of medical specimens.
• Collected data for statistical analysis of all tests.

Education

Coursework in Library Science, University of San Francisco

Medical Laboratory Technology Program, Parkins Community College

Davis License, American Medical Technology Association

B.S. in Biology, University of California, Davis

References will be provided upon request.

Catherine Walker

664 Prospect Avenue
Dover, Delaware 19901
c.walker@xxx.com
(606) 555-5346

Objective   To obtain a position as a special education assistant in a school or residential setting.

Skills
- Team teaching
- Tutoring nursing assistance
- Understanding of emotional, behavioral, and learning disabilities
- Fluent in Spanish

Education   B.A. in Sociology, Delaware State College, 2004
Coursework in Special Education at Delaware State, part-time, working toward an M.A. in Special Education

Member of New England chapter of Association for Children and Adults with Learning Disabilities

Work History   Staff Assistant, Gateway Services, 2005–Present
- Aid professional staff of this residential program for handicapped adults.
- Assist in providing educational services, occupational therapy, and nursing services.

Teacher's Assistant, Elementary School District 58, 2004–2005
- Classroom experience with students affected by emotional and behavioral difficulties and learning disabilities.
- Assisted in preparation and implementation of individualized lesson plans for students.
- Provided progress reports to teacher, parents, and school psychologist.

References Available on Request.

JESSICA LOPEZ

16 Cutriss Street • St. Louis, MO 63105
Jessica.Lopez@xxx.com • (314) 555-8967

Compassionate Nursing • Dedicated Teamwork
Supportive Family Counseling

BACKGROUND

Experienced staff nurse with specialized education and training in serving the health care needs of elderly clients. Currently seeking employment in a geriatric residential or day care facility. Previous employment in hospital, clinic, and home health situations. Teaching experience.

EMPLOYMENT HISTORY

Visiting Nurse, 2004 - Present
Elder Support Services of St. Louis, St. Louis, MO

Staff Nurse, 2002 - 2004
Kingston Clinic, St. Louis, MO

Instructor, 1998 - 2002
Adams College B.S.N. Program, Elmhurst, IL

Staff Nurse, 1992 - 1998
Bethany General Hospital, Oak Park, IL

EDUCATION AND LICENSURE

B.S.N., Northern Illinois University, Dekalb, IL
Registered Nurse, licensed in the states of Illinois and Missouri

ACHIEVEMENTS

- Supervise staff of 12 LPNs and nursing assistants for home health care agency
- Provide emotional support for patient families and referral to appropriate agencies
- Managed large, diverse caseload at urban health clinic
- Participated in ongoing curriculum design and evaluation for B.S.N. program
- Developed and facilitated educational in-service programs for hospital medical staff

References Available

TYRELL DAVIS

1811 Green Street
Cleveland, Ohio 44122
(216) 555-7837 - Cellular
(216) 555-3659 - Home

OBJECTIVE

Position in criminal corrections leading to supervisory/administrative work.

EDUCATION

Ohio State University, B.A. Degree, 2003
Major: Criminal Justice
Minors: Social Service and Political Science

EMPLOYMENT

Cleveland Youth Authority, Corrections Department, Parole Division
Parole Officer (2003 - Present)
Duties:
- Supervise parole procedures for Cleveland Boys School
  and Ohio Youth Correctional Center.
- Prepare home evaluations, social histories, and interviews with inmates.
- Assess inmates' social problems; supervise juvenile offenders;
  counsel inmates and their families.
- Arrange residence, education, and employment for prospective parolees.
- Represent Cleveland Youth Authority at community functions and hearings.
- Act as community liaison.
- Prosecute parole violators.

REFERENCES

Reference available from current supervisor, Walter Reed, (216) 555-7839.

Detailed references upon request.

Roger Boyd

673 Drake Street • Pittsburgh, PA 15234
Home: 412-555-6453 • Cell: 412-555-9834
Email: Roger.Boyd@xxx.com

Job Objective	A legal position with a social service agency
Employment	2004–Present Assistant District Attorney, District Attorney's Office, Pittsburgh, PA Criminal Courts Division • Take depositions from witnesses and complainants • Prepare cases for trial: legal research and writing, filing of motions
	2001–2004 Law Clerk, Morgan & Ryan Legal Corporation, Pittsburgh, PA • Interviewed clients for attorneys • Filed court documents • Standardized manual office procedures • Created interoffice computer networking systems
	1991–2001 Caseworker II, Warren County Department of Social Services, Warren, PA • Established family eligibility for food stamps, public aid, Medicare, and other programs • Maintained average caseload of 75–125 clients at a time
Education	B.A., Sociology, University of Pittsburgh

References Available on Request

Margaret Chang, *Psychiatric Social Worker*

1483 Kathleen Court • Westport, CT 06880 • 203-555-4523 • m.chang@xxx.com

Summary

Trained psychiatric social worker comfortable in a variety of settings, experienced in dealing with diverse client population, seeking new opportunities to assist clients with social and psychiatric adjustment needs.

Work History

Home Health Caseworker
Lutheran Social Services of New England, 2001 to Present
- Provide comprehensive discharge planning for patients leaving Lutheran Community Hospital.
- Refer patients to appropriate community services and programs for nursing, childcare, housekeeping, counseling, and other ongoing needs.

Intake Counselor
Wheeler Psychiatric Institute, 1997 to 2001
- Conducted initial interviews with patients and family members.
- Explained the Institute's programs and fees, patient's rights and responsibilities.
- Assisted patients and family members with decision to admit.
- Referred patients to appropriate community services.

Counselor
Westport Women's Center, 1995 to 1997
- Provided private counseling for area women related to personal and career goals.
- Developed support groups for women dealing with issues of substance abuse and incest survival.

Education

M.S.W, Columbia School of Social Work
B.A., Boston College; Major: Psychology

Skills

- Strong computer skills including database and records management
- Fluent in Chinese and French
- Knowledge of Sign Language

References available upon request

Gary King

33 Elm Street
Jackson, MS 39216
Gary.King@xxx.com
601-555-9076

Counseling Experience

Jackson Memorial Hospital, Jackson, MS
Crisis Counselor, 2001–Present
- Provide crisis intervention and emergency counseling for patients and families.
- Assist hospital personnel and local authorities with suspected child abuse cases.
- Refer patients to social service agencies for grief counseling, hospice care, substance abuse treatment, and other services.
- Design individual discharge plans for psychiatric patients.

Glendale Nursing Pavilion, Jackson, MS
Counseling Specialist, 1997–2001
- Administered psychiatric evaluations to new patients.
- Organized and conducted support groups for residents' family members.
- Provided counseling for residents.
- Arranged educational seminars for staff.

Education

B.S., Human Services, Columbia University, New York
M.S.W. in progress, Mississippi State University, Starkville
Courses:
- Hospital Law
- Enforcement Policies
- AIDS Awareness
- Elder Abuse
- Theories of Group Therapy
- Women and Substance Abuse

Skills

- Familiar with Microsoft Office and numerous other software programs
- C.P.R. Certification
- Conversant in Spanish and Italian

References

Mary Romano, Director, In-Patient Mental Health,
Jackson Memorial Hospital, 601-555-7969

Gary Oldes, Director, Glendale Nursing Pavilion, 601-555-8903

Roberta Morise

67 Gray Street
Marietta, Georgia 30067
404-555-4738 (office)
404-555-2378 (cellular)
Roberta.Morise@xxx.com

Community/Recreation Services Professional

Vocational and Personal Counseling
Youth Recreational Services
Community-Based Social Services

Qualifications

- Extensive paid and volunteer experience with range of community organizations
- Previous positions in public sector and private, not-for-profit groups
- Demonstrated excellence in program design and implementation, counseling, fundraising, and supervision of volunteers

Key Skills

- Publicity
- Supervision
- Desktop Publishing
- Office Management
- Bookkeeping
- Counseling

Employment

Director, Junior Achievement of Georgia (2002 - Present)
- Establish and manage Junior Achievement programs in Georgia schools
- Coordinate publicity efforts
- Recruit volunteer project directors
- Solicit funds from local business leaders
- Compile statistics and project summaries for national office

Day Care Coordinator, Grove Street YMCA, Marietta (1998 - 2002)
- Supervised preschool and summer camp programs
- Assisted in hiring of instructors and camp counselors
- Trained and monitored new counselors
- Supervised production of publicity materials
- Coordinated registration

Employment (continued)
Guidance/Vocation Counselor, Marietta Public High School (1995 - 1998)
• Counseled students regarding personal and educational issues
• Assisted with course scheduling and college entrance planning
• Administered vocational testing
• Assisted director of work/study program

Volunteer Work
Board Member: Marietta Women's Club, Marietta Public Library

Volunteer: St. Theresa's Homeless Shelter

Education
M.S. in Counseling, University of Virginia
B.S. in History, Mississippi State University

References available on request

■ ■ Omar Hasak

17 Dayton Street
Tempe, AZ 85281
O.Hasak@xxx.com
602-555-8057

■ Overview

Secondary school principal and former teacher with 12 years of
experience. Extensive background in budgets, community relations,
teacher contract negotiations.

■ Capabilities

- ■ Administration of large public and private high schools.
- ■ Principal of 1,500-student suburban public high school; former
  principal of 1,200-student private academy.
- ■ Supervision of teachers and school staff.
- ■ Supervised 80 unionized public high school teachers.
- ■ Directed staff of 65 teachers and other personnel at private
  academy.
- ■ Preparation and management of $1–$6 million school budgets.
- ■ Successful fundraising drives and grant proposals to fund new
  construction and repair of existing facilities.
- ■ Curriculum design for new computer literacy program for high
  school district.
- ■ District representative for teacher contract negotiations.
- ■ Four years' experience as high school English instructor.

■ Experience

Principal, Maine County High School, Tempe, AZ, 8/00 to Present

Principal, St. Vincent's Academy, Yuma, AZ, 1/95 to 5/00

English Instructor, Alamar High School, Houston, TX, 9/91 to 1/95

■ Education

M.S., Public School Administration, 12/94
Arizona State University, Tempe, AZ

B.A., English, 5/91
Southern Methodist University, Dallas, TX

■ Publications

"Computer Literacy and Facilities Design," *Curriculum Review*, vol. 81, March 2005

"The Multicultural Classroom," *Instructor*, vol. 21, number 2, January 2006

■ Relevant Information

- ■ Personal desire to relocate to Scottsdale area.
- ■ Willing to travel to Scottsdale for personal interview.
- ■ Available Fall 2006.

■ References

Excellent professional references available upon request.

Terrence Johnson

14 Randall Road
Atlanta, GA 30315
T.Johnson@xxx.com
404-759-9463

Job Objective	Camp counselor position for the summer of 2006
Education	University of Alabama, B.S. degree in progress Expected graduation date: June 2007 Major: Psychology/Child Development Minor: Recreation and Leisure
Certifications	Red Cross–trained and certified swimming instructor CPR certified
Employment	Counselor, Junior Adventure Camp, Summer 2005 *Supervised, with 3 other counselors, a group of 50 children, ages 7 to 10, at park district day camp. Led games, explained craft projects, supervised field trips and weekly visits to the local water park.* Day Care Worker, Kid's Place, 2004 - 2005 *Worked 15 hours per week during sophomore year at local day care center. Responsible for playground supervision, recreational activities, and routine care of children aged 6 months to 5 years.* Swimming Instructor, Water World, Summer 2004 *Swimming instructor in Red Cross–approved swimming program for ages 4 to 10. Planned and conducted swimming lessons, evaluated students for proper class assignment, acted as lifeguard.*

References furnished upon request

JOHN PARKER, NUTRITIONIST

17 Oak Lane • Omaha, Nebraska 61855 • 402-555-6579
John.Parker@xxx.com

WORK HISTORY

Chief Dietician
St. Vincent's Hospital • 483 Prentiss Circle • Omaha, Nebraska
Dates: 6/98 to Present
• Perform budget development and approval.
• Plan menus and supervise patient food preparation.
• Supervise food procurement.
• Interact with medical staff to develop individualized diets that assist
  patient's recovery.
• Assure compliance with health and safety codes.

Dietitian
Terrence Community College • 653 Rogers Parkway • Omaha, Nebraska
Dates: 7/95 to 6/98
• Planned menus and supervised food preparation for food services
  department.
• Prepared daily meals and catered for special events on campus.
• Participated in plans for redesign and expansion of student cafeteria.

EDUCATION

B.S., Nutrition, Northern Illinois University, 1995
Honors: Dean's List last three years

REFERENCES

Available on Request.

Ernesto Jones

64 West 62nd Street, #3B
Brooklyn, New York 11210
E.Jones@xxx.com
212-555-8935

Experience

2000 - present
New York Department of Public Aid, Senior Caseworker
1997 - 2000
Brooklyn Social Services Administration, Caseworker
1995 - 1997
Brooklyn Department of Veterans' Affairs, Benefits Specialist

Abilities

- Thorough knowledge of eligibility requirements for New York State public welfare programs
- Experience handling large, complex caseloads
- Knowledge of Spanish and Sign Language
- Ability to conduct accurate eligibility investigations
- Strong interpersonal, organizational, and interviewing skills
- Supervisory experience
- Community relation skills

Education

M.S.W., New York University, 1997
B.A., Psychology, Boston College, 1994

References available upon request

Grace Miller
615 Robin Lane • Toledo, Ohio 43604 • G.Miller@xxx.com • 419-555-4803

Objective
Position as a music therapist

Background
- Talented, degreed professional with eight years' experience
- Excellent singer, pianist, guitarist
- Comfortable with clients/students of all ages and backgrounds
- Resourceful and compassionate care and instruction

Employment
Music Therapist, 9/99 to Present
Rockdale Nursing Center/Toledo, Ohio
- Direct recreational and therapeutic music activities at this 500-bed, long-term care facility
- Assess patients' needs
- Conduct group music activities
- Perform for patients and staff
- Arrange for musical presentations by local choirs, school groups, and professional musicians

Assistant Music Director, 6/99 to 9/99
Toledo Summer Arts/Toledo, Ohio
- Assisted music director at this summer camp for young musicians
- Provided information and tours for prospective students and their families
- Designed and supervised group musical activities

Music Teacher, 9/92 to 6/99
Shultz Junior High School/Toledo, Ohio
- Taught music education classes
- Directed choir
- Produced, directed, and publicized large-scale holiday performance each year
- Served as vocal coach for annual variety show

Education
M.A., Ohio State University, 1999
Major: Music Therapy

B.A., Kenyon College, 1992
Major: Music
Minor: Psychology

References
Will be provided upon request

MARRIETTA SUAREZ
73 Carriage Court
Oklahoma City, OK 73106
m.suarez@xxx.com
(405) 555-5894

CAREER GOAL
Supervisory position in physical therapy

EXPERIENCE
Director, Department of Physical Therapy, 1999–Present
Oklahoma Rehabilitation Institute
❭ Supervise 10 staff members, including physical therapists, aides, and support staff
❭ Develop patient therapy programs
❭ Attend interdisciplinary staff meetings to coordinate patient care with other hospital departments
❭ Consult with medical staff as necessary
❭ Make recommendations to hospital board regarding departmental budget, equipment purchases, facilities design, long-range planning
❭ Assist in hiring and training new personnel

Physical Therapist, 1996–1999
Bethany Christian Hospital
❭ Assisted stroke and accident victims and other patients in recovery of range of motion
❭ Provided postoperative physical therapy
❭ Assisted patients with adjustment to prosthetic limbs
❭ Conducted patient and family education

Physical Therapy Aide, 1994–1996
McHenry County Veterans Hospital
❭ Assisted physical therapists with all aspects of patient care
❭ Extensive charting and record keeping

CREDENTIALS
Board Certified Physical Therapist, trained at University of Oklahoma
Member, American Physical Therapy Association

REFERENCES
Will be provided upon request

JOE SABATINI
1650 Newland Lane
Sioux Falls, SD 57105
joe.sabatini@xxx.com
(605) 555-7348

JOB EXPERIENCE
Sioux Falls Police Department
Patrolman, 8/96 - Present
- Foot patrol, radio car patrol, dispatch officer, special security assignment at Sioux Falls High School.
- Police photographer for accident investigations.
- Radio dispatch instructor for new members of force.
- Implemented community policing policy.
- Recognized, respected member of local community.
- Received two Distinguished Service awards.

Pittsburgh Police Department
Assistant to Director, Domestic Violence Unit, 8/94 - 8/96
- Handled domestic disturbance calls.
- Provided community referral and crisis counseling for families involved.
- Filed reports and maintained records.
- Compiled statistics.
- Provided expert and eye witness testimony in court.
- Did public speaking on issue of domestic violence.

EDUCATION
B.A. in Sociology, 1994
Pennsylvania State University

Police Academy Training Course, 1996
University of Pittsburgh

MEMBERSHIPS
Police Athletic League, Sioux Falls
Fraternal Order of Police, Sioux Falls Chapter

References Available on Request.

Patricia Kelly
17 Woods Rd.
Frederick, MD 21702
301-555-3495 (Cellular)
patricia.kelly@xxx.com

Background

Experienced academic administrator with demonstrated ability in key areas of financial management, teacher supervision, curriculum development, and community relations.

Administrative Experience

School Superintendent, Crawford High School, Frederick, MD
January 1995 to Present
Supervise faculty of 700 teachers. Manage budget of $75 million. Accomplishments include construction of two new elementary schools, implementation of successful bus safety program adopted by other cities, best student/teacher ratio in the state, student test scores in the top 5 percent of national ratings, ongoing teacher enrichment programs.

Principal, Wakefield Academy, Baltimore, MD
September 1991 to December 1994
Participated in staff hiring, training, and evaluation. Financial management of school, including direction of fundraising efforts. Oversaw curriculum development and textbook adoptions. Interacted with school board, PTA, and community groups. Supervised marketing campaign that increased school enrollment by 7 percent. Designed in-service programs for teaching staff.

Counseling Experience

Guidance Counselor, Bethesda High School, Bethesda, MD
September 1988 to June 1991
Provided personal and academic counseling to high school students. As college admissions advisor, arranged college fair that allowed seniors to meet with admissions representatives from 15 colleges. Seventy-five percent of counselees attended first-choice college. Managed work/study program. Designed and implemented Graduation First, a program of personal/academic counseling, flexible scheduling, and work/study options to assist at-risk students and lower the dropout rate.

Teaching Experience

Reading Instructor, North Ridge High School, Bethesda, MD
August 1986 to June 1988

Substitute Teacher, Clarke County School District, Clarke County, MD
August 1985 to June 1986

Education

M.Ed. School Administration, University of Virginia

B.A. Education, Penn State University

Detailed references will be furnished upon request.

Liz Newson

3 Lee Road, Santa Barbara, CA 93101

NEWSON ASSOCIATES
Counseling & Alternative Medicine
Phone 805-555-8594
Hours: Mon - Fri 8 - 4 & evenings by appointment

Services

- Individual and group counseling for personal growth, academic progress, health and wellness, career decision making and advancement
- Hypnotherapy to resolve substance abuse, compulsive disorders, and other issues requiring behavioral modification
- Relaxation and stress management programs for groups and individuals (in my offices or on-site)
- Biofeedback for treatment of stress and sleep disorders
- Acupuncture and herbal treatment for stress management
- Assertiveness training seminars for women

Clients

Consultant, UCLA Department of Psychology
Speaker/Consultant, Triton Holistic Health Center
Therapist/Owner, Newson Associates

Education and Training

M.A. in Clinical Psychology, University of California
B.A. in Psychology, Augustana College
California Acupuncture License
State Certification in Hypnotherapy

Memberships

American Group Psychotherapy Association
California Mental Health Association

References Available Upon Request

BRUCE WILSON

740 Carthage Court • Lake Forest, Illinois 60045
847-555-4857 home • 847-555-1421 cellular

WORK HISTORY

Cook County Juvenile Detention Center, Chicago, Illinois
Educational Director, 2002–Present
- Interact with local school districts, social workers, criminal justice officials, and juvenile offenders
- Design group and individual instruction programs
- Hire, train, and evaluate instructors for the program
- Evaluate student progress and adjust curriculum as necessary

Stevenson Youth House, Milwaukee, Wisconsin
Director, 1999–2002
- Managed supervised living facility for 20 at-risk adolescent males
- Provided educational and cultural enrichment programs
- Supervised staff of three
- Responsible for all aspects of financial management
- Provided counseling and employment opportunities for residents

Tacoma Juvenile Correctional Center, Tacoma, Washington
Probation Aide, 1996–1999
- Maintained records on juvenile offenders
- Researched case histories and conducted interviews
- Presented written progress reports and recommendations to judicial authorities
- Conducted investigations to assist in apprehension of parole violators

EDUCATION

Master's Degree in Criminal Justice, 1999
Northern Illinois University, DeKalb

Bachelor's Degree in Education and Psychology, 1996
University of Illinois, Urbana-Champaign

LANGUAGES

Fluent in French and Spanish
Conversant in Italian

References Available Upon Request

John A. Stevens

422 Kenmore Drive • Sarasota, FL 33581

John.Stevens@xxx.com • (813) 555-3958

JOB OBJECTIVE

A paramedic position

EXPERIENCE

Paramedic, 2001 - Present
Sarasota Fire Department, Ambulance Rescue Division
Duties:
- Respond to emergency medical calls.
- Assess patients' medical conditions in field and relay status to hospital emergency staff.
- Transport patients to area hospitals.
- Provide basic and advanced life support per physician's phone instructions while en route to hospital.

Key Skills: Vital signs check, CPR, defibrillation, intubation, administration of medication, shock prevention.

EMT, 1997 - 2001
Regency Ambulance Service (private ambulance company)
Duties:
- Took vital signs and provided basic life support.
- Transported patients to area hospitals.

Key Skills: Maintenance of airway, provision of oxygen, bleeding control, shock prevention.

EMT, 1994 - 1997
Sarasota General Hospital, Emergency Department
Duties:
- Assisted emergency medical staff in providing direct patient care.

Key Skills: Vital signs check, phlebotomy, EKG.

EDUCATION

Sarasota Community College, Associate Degree/Biology, 1994
- Emergency Medical Technician Courses, I & II
- Advanced Cardiac Life Support (ACLS) Certification
- CPR Certification

REFERENCES

Jack Smith, Fire Chief
Sarasota Fire Department
813-555-9845

Barbara Evans, Nurse Clinician
Sarasota General Hospital
813-555-6735

Anthony Berelli, EMT Supervisor
Regency Ambulance Service
813-555-7845

MIRA SURESH

Registered Nurse
1640 Ashfield Road
Nashville, TN 37204
615-555-7896
M.Suresh@xxx.com

EMPLOYMENT

United Home Health Care, Nashville, TN
Registered Nurse, 2000–Present

St. Francis Hospital, Atlanta, GA
Staff Nurse, 1995–2000

Davis Family Clinic, Atlanta, GA
Registered Nurse, 1996–1999

SKILLS

Home Health Professional: Able to review history, assess patients' needs and provide appropriate level of care. Cases have included pediatric through geriatric patients. Recent patients have included accident, burn, surgery, stroke, heart attack, and AIDS patients. Comfortable using oxygen, IVs, traction, and other medical equipment in home setting.

Experienced Staff Nurse: Responsible for all aspects of patient care. Took patient histories, kept charts. Monitored patients' progress and administered medications and treatment. Explained procedures and home care to patients and their families. Briefed staff on patient status.

EDUCATION

B.S.N. from the University of Georgia, 1996
State Board Certification in Georgia and Tennessee

REFERENCES AVAILABLE

James Thiros
450 Merrill Drive • Austin, TX 78702
j.thiros@xxx.com • (512) 555-8965

Career Goal   Position in elementary education

Experience   Fifth Grade Teacher, Woodland Elementary School
Austin, TX, 2001 - Present
- Responsible for classes of 20–25 fifth graders for past five years
- Teach core curriculum: English, math, science, and social science
- Work with music, art, and other teachers to coordinate curriculum
- Administer national academic progress tests
- Represent teachers on district's curriculum review board
- Organize and direct annual science fair

Fourth Grade Teacher, Jefferson Elementary School
Austin, TX, 1999 - 2001
- Responsible for fourth grade classes of 18–22 students
- Taught core curriculum
- Participated in long-range curriculum planning, reviewing such issues as textbook adoptions and combined classroom concept
- Organized fundraising drive to fund expanded computer learning center, including candy sales and direct community fundraising
- Organized and supervised field trips

Education   M.A., Elementary Education/Texas Certification
Rice University, Houston, TX

B.S., Education/Biology, Grades 1–6
Concordia University, Austin, TX

Professional Affiliations   • National Education Association
- Parent Teachers Association
- Texas Teachers Association
- Texas Hellenic Youth Council, Youth Education Committee Member

References available upon request

Warren Deveroe

118 W. 86th St., #3C
New York, NY 10024
(212) 555-7635 cellular
warren.deveroe@xxx.com

Specialization

Nonprofit fundraising and marketing consultant

Capabilities

Experienced in all aspects of direct mail campaigns
Design, write, and produce informational and fundraising letters and
 brochures
Manage telemarketing campaigns
Conduct market research
Write press releases for radio, TV, newspapers, and magazines
Degrees in business and marketing
Eight years as successful business consultant

Clients

National Public Radio
World Wildlife Federation
Special Olympics
Mothers Against Drunk Drivers
Cancer Federation
Americans for International Aid

Education

Villanova University
M.B.A./Financial Management

Queens College
B.S./Business with emphasis in Marketing

References will be furnished upon request

LISA DENORELLI

1611 Margaret Street
Scranton, PA 18505
(717) 555-4983 (Office)
(717) 555-4094 (Home)

OBJECTIVE:
Management of nonprofit social service agency

CURRENT POSITION:
Director, Susan's Place, Scranton, PA, 2002–Present
Community Social Service Agency for Women, providing the following
services:
- Legal Aid
- Day Care
- Job Training
- Food Pantry
- Homeless Shelter
- Counseling and Referral

Duties include:
- Bookkeeping
- Staffing
- Program Design
- Community Outreach
- Fundraising
- Long-Range Planning

PREVIOUS POSITIONS:
Media Specialist, AIDS Action Committee, Pittsburgh, PA, 1999–2002

Fundraiser, Children's Welfare League, Los Angeles, CA, 1998–1999

Researcher, Center for Domestic Violence Research, Oakland, CA,
1996–1998

EDUCATION:
M.S.W. from the University of Massachusetts, Amherst, MA

B.A. in English from Mills College, Oakland, CA

REFERENCES:
Available on Request

Darrell Simpson

60 Stevens Parkway
Chapel Hill, NC 27514
(919) 555-0979
Darrell.Simpson@xxx.com

Objective

Position with a recreation or social service agency that will allow me to
continue to serve youth.

Work History

Program Director, 2002 - Present
Outward Bound, Chapel Hill, NC
Organize and supervise trips (one day to one week) for teens. Program
teaches wilderness survival skills, self-reliance, self-esteem, group
interdependence. Arrange all aspects of trips, including assisting with
advertising, scouting locations, preparing sites, supervising registration
and transportation, designing and directing activities. Recruit and train
new volunteers. Expanded program participation 15 percent.

Youth Coordinator, 1999 - 2002
The Wilderness Society, Seattle, WA
Developed program of nature appreciation and conservancy for children
and teens. Designed Outdoor Adventure, guided walks at area nature
preserves for elementary students. Coordinated with National Park
Service to set up education centers at two local parks. Led Wilderness
Teen Camp backpacking, canoeing, and camping trips designed to
improve fitness, self-confidence, and environmental awareness.

Activities Director, 1997 - 1999
Camp Wichita, Wichita, KS
Designed and supervised on-site recreational activities and day trips
for more than 120 campers ages 5 to 10. Trained, supervised, and
evaluated counselors.

Education/Certifications

B.A., Leisure and Recreation, University of North Carolina
Red Cross First Aid and Swimming Certifications

References Available

Rhonda Morgan

16 Easton Court
Salt Lake City, UT 84116
(801) 555-9987

Professional Experience

Owner/Operator, Wee Care Day School, 1997 - Present
Salt Lake City, UT
- Own and operate day care center serving up to 25 children, ages 1–5 years.
- Direct three highly qualified teachers and office manager in providing routine care, educational development opportunities, and social interaction for children.
- Maintain a modern facility with fully equipped nap center, changing station, classroom/playroom, outdoor play area, and small lunchroom.
- Excellent record of safety and customer satisfaction.
- Client list available.

Assistant Director, Child Care Program, NUA Business Systems, 1995 - 1997
Salt Lake City, UT
- Assisted director of on-site day care center operated for employees of NUA.
- Interacted with children, teachers, parents, and company management to meet the needs of 40 children in full-day and before/after school programs.
- Organized and directed activities.
- Administered routine care and first aid (as necessary).

Teacher's Aide, Kensington Montessori School, 1994 - 1995
Salt Lake City, UT
- Assisted preschool teacher at local Montessori school.
- Conducted games and activities designed to improve children's fine motor skills, self-expression, social skills, and educational preparedness.
- Participated in teacher/parent conferences and staff meetings.

Professional Credentials

Associate Degree, Early Childhood Education, Salt Lake City Community College

Licensed Child Care Worker, Utah Board of Commissioners

CPR/First Aid Certification

Member, National Association of Child Care Professionals

Detailed references will be furnished upon request.

• Amy Ryan •
Nonprofit Public Information Specialist

1450 Magnolia Lane
Lemon Grove, California 92045
(805) 555-5678
A.Ryan@xxx.com

• Goal

Public information position in nonprofit health care organization that
utilizes my strong writing and public relations skills.

• Work History

American Cancer Society, Goletta, California
Public Information Specialist, 2001–Present
- Design, write, and produce major publications including monthly
  newsletter, annual report, and fundraising brochures.
- Write press releases and act as liaison between ACS and media,
  including newspaper, television, and radio journalists.
- Arrange press conferences at request of Public Information Director.

Parkland General Hospital, Ventura, California
Public Information Intern, 1999–2000
- Wrote and edited press releases for local media.
- Developed, researched, and wrote articles for quarterly magazine.
- Wrote and edited speeches for hospital board members.
- Produced copy and acquired photos for fundraising brochures.

• Education

B.A. Degree/Public Relations, 2000
University of California, Los Angeles, California

References Available on Request.

helena shapiro ◆ ◆ ◆

86 Wayland Court • Boulder, Colorado 80205 • (303) 555-9085
Helena.Shapiro@xxx.com

experience

Docent and Educator, Denver Museum of Art, 2003–Present
- ◆ Conduct educational tours of museum for elementary grades.
- ◆ Direct Young Masters Program and summer and weekend courses in drawing, painting, and sculpture for gifted students.

Private Art Teacher (part-time), 2002–2005
- ◆ Offered private instruction in painting and drawing from my home studio.
- ◆ Specialized in ages 5–15.

Art Teacher, Richardson Elementary School, 2000–2003
- ◆ Taught art education courses to grades K–6.
- ◆ Organized art contests within school and student submissions to district and statewide contests.
- ◆ Assisted students in producing sets and props for annual variety show.
- ◆ Interacted with students, staff, teachers, parents, and PTA.

education

B.A. in Art History/Elementary Education, 2000
University of Colorado, Boulder, Colorado

References Available.

Diego Vasquez

715 Conway Court • Santa Fe, NM 85702 • (505) 555-4958 • D.Vasquez@xxx.com

Athletic Training/Coaching

Basketball Coach/Santa Fe Community High School/Santa Fe
• Coach high school basketball team with winning record in conference.
• Determine strategy; teach players specific formations and general skills.
• Provide psychological motivation.
• Supervise team during games.
• Good rapport with players, officials, school administrators, and parents.
• Emphasis on developing fitness and good sportsmanship.

Personal Trainer/Valley Fitness Center/Santa Fe
• Designed individual fitness programs that were safe yet challenging.
• Motivated clients to continue with fitness regimen.
• Developed online workout logs for clients and a chat room to discuss all aspects of fitness training.

Teaching

Physical Education Teacher/Santa Fe Community High School/Santa Fe
• Teach Boys and Girls Physical Education courses.
• Responsible for teaching diverse core curriculum, including swimming, baseball, basketball, tennis, and volleyball.
• Assist athletic director with schoolwide fitness testing program

Aerobics Instructor/Valley Fitness Center/Santa Fe
• Taught both low- and high-impact aerobics.
• Designed routines and selected music.
• Taught students self-monitoring skills to ensure a safe workout.

Employers

Santa Fe Community High School, Santa Fe	2003 - present
Valley Fitness Center, Santa Fe	2001 - 2004
Community Swim Center, Santa Barbara	Summers/1996 - 2001

Education

B.A./Physical Education/University of California/Santa Barbara
Secondary Teaching Certification/New Mexico and California

Red Cross–Certified Swimming Instructor

References available upon request.

INA PAUL

83 Silver Spring Road
Anchorage, AK 99503

(907) 555-5960
Ina.Paul@xxx.com

SUMMARY

Private psychotherapist with successful practice for past five years in individual and group therapy. Previous experience in health care and business settings. Proven record of success at teaching clients behavioral modification techniques. Training and experience with 12-step system.

PROFESSIONAL SKILLS

- Dealing with eating disorders, including anorexia nervosa, bulimia, and morbid obesity
- Substance abuse strategies, including 12-step methods and support groups for alcohol and drug addiction recovery
- Crisis counseling and interventions for families of substance abusers
- Referral to appropriate community and health care services as necessary
- Tracing progress and coordinating counseling and recovery strategies for patients hospitalized for treatment
- Public speaking engagements to address issues of substance abuse and eating disorders

EDUCATION

M.A., Clinical Psychology, University of Alaska, Anchorage
B.A., Sociology, Alaska Pacific University

EMPLOYMENT HISTORY

Private Practice, 2000–present
Anchorage

Counselor, 1998–2000
Bristol Clinic (private clinic, substance abuse recovery), Anchorage

Counselor, 1996–1998
Diet Center Inc., Juneau

LANGUAGES

Conversant in a number of native dialects

REFERENCES

References will be furnished on request

➣ *Hannah Colgan*

4215 Ridge Road
Washington, DC 90210
Hannah.Colgan@xxx.com
(202) 555-3959

Areas of Expertise

➣ Residential counseling for at-risk adolescents
➣ Chemical dependency assessment and treatment
➣ Eating disorder assessment and treatment
➣ Grief therapy for clients recovering from a death, divorce, or other loss
➣ Marital counseling and conflict resolution techniques
➣ Crisis counseling and treatment of clinical depression

Education and Training

B.A., Psychology
Georgetown University, Washington, DC

M.A., Counseling
University of Wisconsin, Madison, WI

Certificate, Grief Therapy
Loyola College, Montreal

Work History

Consultant, 2002–Present
Brookside Group Home, Washington, DC
➣ Serve as mental health consultant to residential program for
   adolescents at risk.
➣ Consult with staff members on cases as requested.
➣ Conduct group therapy sessions for emotionally troubled teens.
➣ Attend monthly staff meetings.
➣ Participate in fundraising efforts and long-range planning.

Work History (continued)

Therapist/Co-Owner, 2000–Present
Wilson, Colgan & Stevenson Mental Health Associates, Washington, DC
➤ Partner in private mental health practice.
➤ Maintain current patient load of 60{plus} patients in ongoing
   individual and group therapy dealing with personal, marital,
   substance abuse, and other issues.
➤ Monitor and record patient progress.
➤ Attend weekly staff meeting.
➤ Provide referral services.

Substance Abuse Specialist, 1997–2000
Conlin Clinic, Bethesda, MD
➤ Took patients' histories and assessed patients' needs.
➤ Provided details of substance abuse program to patients and families.
➤ Conducted tours of facility for prospective patients and families.
➤ Helped patients adjust to clinic.
➤ Provided individual and group counseling.
➤ Monitored patient progress.
➤ Assisted patients with discharge planning.
➤ Instituted family support group.

Community Service

Volunteer
St. Paul's Suicide Prevention Hotline, Washington, DC

Member, Board of Directors
Nicolet Mental Health Center, Bethesda, MD

References Available.

TIMOTHY VAUGHN

450 King Drive • Bennington, CT 48009 • (203) 555-5948

Timothy.Vaughn@xxx.com

WORK HISTORY

Landscape Architect, 2001 - Present
City of Bennington, CT
• Design public parks and recreational areas within the city
• Work with government and community groups to coordinate
  preservation efforts and address environmental concerns
• Research land use and provide written reports to city government
• Provide project suggestions and estimated budgets to city planning
  officials
• Supervise routine park maintenance and park enhancement projects
• Purchase park maintenance equipment

Supervisor, 1998 - 2001
Grove Nursery, Montgomery, AL
• Hired, trained, and supervised nursery staff
• Selected subcontractors and negotiated prices and delivery schedules
• Purchased and maintained all equipment
• Supervised landscaping projects for clients, including ground
  maintenance and installation of gardens, borders, and annual displays

EDUCATION

B.S., Landscape Architecture, University of Alabama, 1997
Licensed Landscape Contractor

REFERENCES AVAILABLE

YOLANDA ORTEGA

655 Ashland Drive

Irvine, California 92714

(714) 555-9587 home

(714) 555-6453 cellular

OBJECTIVE

Social service position with supervisory potential

EDUCATION

University of California, Santa Barbara

M.S.W., 2000

B.A., Sociology, 1996

SKILLS

- Research applicants' eligibility for social services and approve or deny claims
- Manage large caseloads in timely and compassionate manner in accordance with agency guidelines
- Interview social service applicants and inform them of their rights and responsibilities
- Provide referral to other community agencies as appropriate
- Bilingual - Spanish/English - able to translate legal and other complex documents and interpret for Hispanic clients
- Excellent clerical and organizational skills
- Knowledge of Word, Excel, Access, and PowerPoint

EMPLOYMENT

2002–Present

Caseworker, Los Angeles County Social Services

2000–2002

Medical Social Worker, Los Angeles Office of Veterans Affairs

1996–2000

Administrative Assistant, Los Angeles County Legal Aid Society

REFERENCES

Cecilia Reed, (213) 555-5068

Senior Caseworker, Los Angeles Office of Veterans Affairs

Michael Wu, (213) 555-6079

Attorney, Los Angeles County Legal Aid Society

• Gregory Sansone •

17 Sandstone Court
Augusta, Georgia 30901
Greg.Sansone@xxx.com
(404) 555-9684

• • •

• Employment

July 2003 to present
Deputy Sheriff, Augusta, Georgia
- General law enforcement duties, including supervision of police officers and staff, traffic control, accident investigation, crowd control, cooperation with state and federal authorities on criminal investigations.

January 2000 to June 2003
Detective, Atlanta Police Department
- Responsible for electronic and other surveillance of criminal suspects, including pursuit of suspects and documentation of their whereabouts.
- Knowledge of evidence collection and video and photo surveillance.
- Familiar with pertinent civil and criminal statutes.

September 1999 to December 1999
Special Investigator, Atlanta Police Department
- Hired on temporary basis to assist with undercover drug investigation.
- Assisted officers with surveillance and relevant data entry.
- Provided courtroom testimony for investigation leading to four arrests and convictions.

• Education

B.S., Criminal Justice, Georgia State University, 1999

Atlanta Police Training Institute Certification
- Evidence Technician
- Narcotics Investigation
- Surveillance Techniques

References Available Upon Request.

Sheila Ryan

73 Wisconsin Street
Portland, OR 97219
503-555-3958
Sheila.Ryan@xxx.com

Objective

A responsible position as a political aide

Key Skills
- Fundraising
- Public Speaking
- Speech Writing
- Office Management
- Research

Job Experience

Office of Congresswoman Mary Martin/Office Manager/2003 to Present
- Compile statistics and write weekly status reports
- Attend staff meetings
- Supervise office staff, including training, scheduling, and evaluation
- Draft responses to constituents' letters
- Assist with fundraising efforts
- Write and present speeches on congresswoman's policies to women's and community groups

Office of Assemblyman Walter Smith/Office Assistant/2000 to 2003
- Responded to constituents' concerns
- Performed heavy telephone and correspondence duties
- Wrote campaign brochure and press releases

Volunteer Work

League of Women Voters/Assistant to Educational Director/1999 to 2000

Amnesty International/Active Member/1999 to Present

Education

B.S., Political Science
University of Wisconsin–Madison

References on Request

EDITH KRAVITZ

4820 BRIARCREST DRIVE • RICHMOND, VIRGINIA 23226
(804) 555-4859
EDITH.KRAVITZ@xxx.COM

SPECIALIZATION
Academic Counseling

WORK HISTORY
Guidance Counselor, 2000 - present
North Central High School, Richmond, Virginia

Resident Counselor, 2000 - 2002
Clarendon Academy, Richmond, Virginia

English Teacher, 1997 - 2000
Grant High School, Midlothian, Virginia

English Teacher, 1995 - 1997
Emporia High School, Emporia, Virginia

SKILLS
- Admissions and financial aid advice for college-bound juniors and seniors
- Curriculum counseling for high school students
- Organization and supervision of work/study programs
- Individual and group counseling for adolescents to resolve personal problems and improve academic performance
- Study skills, college selection, and resume/job search seminars for students
- Resident advisor for adolescents
- Experienced English instructor

ACCOMPLISHMENTS
- Reduced dropout rate at North Central High (15 percent during last four years)
- Increased student and community business involvement in work/study program
- Awarded PTA Excellence in Education Award, 2005

EDUCATION

Certified School Guidance Counselor, 2000
State of Virginia Board of Education

M.Ed., Guidance and Counseling, 2000
University of New Hampshire

B.A., English, 1995
Boston College

REFERENCES

Marsha Pell, Director
Clarendon Academy
Marsha.Pell@xxx.com
(804) 555-2839

Walter Davis, Principal
North Central High School
W.Davis@xxx.com
(804) 555-3958

KEVIN LEE

■ 1015 Rialto St.
■ Bennington, VT 05201
■ Kevin.Lee@xxx.com
■ 802-695-1213

OBJECTIVE
Hospital Administration

PROFESSIONAL EXPERIENCE

Financial Management
■ Experience preparing and managing annual budgets of up to $15 million
■ Fundraising ability, including soliciting corporate funds and private donations to fund hospital expansion projects
■ Cost-effective resolution of worker compensation claims, employee contracts, and rate negotiation with insurance companies
■ Administration of successful materials cost-containment program that has reduced expenditures for hospital supplies by approximately 20 percent

Personnel Management
■ Development of ongoing nursing recruitment program that increased staffing to 95 percent of required level, with full staffing expected within the next year
■ Implementation of successful community volunteer program
■ Successful labor negotiations and reduction in staff turnover rate of 15 percent
■ Extensive staff development programs and opportunities
■ Strong commitment to continuing education of staff

Marketing and Administration
■ Maintenance of professional standards as evidenced by full accreditation of both hospitals during tenure
■ Direction of successful public information and marketing programs
■ Facilities maintenance and planning, including expansion and updating of hospital facilities

EMPLOYMENT

Bennington Memorial Hospital, Bennington, VT
2002–Present

Georgetown General Hospital, Washington, DC
1997–2002

Page 1 of 2

EDUCATION
B.A., Economics, Columbia University

M.S., Hospital Administration, Georgetown University

AFFILIATIONS
- Consultant, President's Task Force on Health Care Reform
- American Hospital Association
- American Society of Hospital Administrators

REFERENCES
References will be provided on request

MICHAEL WINTERS

304 Harrison Street • Brooklyn, New York 11213
212-555-7609 Office • 212-555-7623 Cell

CAREER GOAL

Management of nonprofit social service agency

WORK HISTORY

Director, AIDS Action Coalition, 2002 - present
Brooklyn, New York

Skills Used:
- Financial Management
- Fundraising
- Research
- Public Education
- Governmental Lobbying
- Public Speaking

Direct the agency as it pursues the goals of achieving public
sensitivity to AIDS and promoting adequate funding for treatment
and research. Manage staff of 10 employees and 30 volunteers.
Direct fundraising efforts. Publish monthly newsletter. Interact
with other community service and health care organizations
striving to meet the needs of persons living with AIDS. Monitor
pertinent state and federal legislation and organize lobbying
efforts. Perform numerous public speaking engagements.

Director, Nessett House, 2000 - 2002
Brooklyn, New York

Skills Used:
- Fundraising
- Financial Management
- Community Outreach
- Substance Abuse Therapy
- Group Therapy
- Conflict Resolution

Resident director at supervised living facility serving residents
recovering from substance abuse and alcohol addiction.
Management of budget and direction of day-to-day operations.
Direction of publicity efforts and fundraising campaigns. Provision
of individual and group substance abuse recovery counseling.

EDUCATION
Coursework in Accounting, 2001
New York University

M.S.W., Counseling and Psychology, 1990
Boston University

B.A., Economics and Psychology, 1986
Rutgers University

REFERENCES
Will be provided on request.

Elizabeth Anne Engle

16 N. Sheffield Rd.
Minneapolis, MN 55429
Liz.Engle@xxx.com
(612) 555-1423

Professional Goal

To utilize my nursing skills in a challenging position in
a professional health care setting

Professional Strengths

- Strong assessment skills for evaluating patients' needs and providing proper referrals to other medical professionals and community support groups
- Proven ability to assist patients and families in developing appropriate coping strategies in response to illness
- Successful experience mediating between staff members and acting as community liaison
- Strong commitment to continuing education and patient advocacy

Education

M.S.N., Community Health, College of Misericordia, 2004

B.S.N., Marywood College, 2000

Previous Positions

Nursing Consultant, Swedish American Hospice, 2003–Present

Pediatric Staff Nurse, Shriners Children's Hospital, 2000–2003

References Available on Request

Amanda Richardson

915 Lake Street, #6B
White Plains, NY 10036
Mandy.Richardson@xxx.com
(914) 555-7934

Excellent six-year record of service to the city of White Plains, New York, in their uniform division. Helped implement community policing policy credited with reducing local crime rate.

Achievements

White Plains Police Department (1999 - 2005)
- Conducted successful robbery and assault investigations leading to approximately 40 arrests.
- Interviewed both suspects and complainants.
- Conducted background checks.
- Organized and participated in community safety awareness programs at local schools and businesses.
- Supervised orientation for new officers.

Awards

Three Distinguished Service Awards (2003, 2004, 2005)
Mayor's Community Service Award (2005)
Certificate of Service, White Plains School District 84 (2004)

Education

New York State Police Academy, 1999
Albany, NY
Graduated with Honors

B.A., Law and Society, 1998
University of California, Los Angeles

References available upon request

JOHANNA BROWN

133 Lincoln Dr. • Detroit, MI 48099
(613) 555-3361 home • (613) 555-8454 mobile

POSITION DESIRED

Health Care Administrator in a hospital or clinic.

EDUCATION

Master of Science Degree, April 1987, Western Michigan University.
Public Health Administration.

Bachelor of Science Degree, April 1983, Western Michigan University.
Major: Business.
Minor: Biology.

EXPERIENCE

1987 - present: Director, Vicksburg Community Hospitals.
Directed operation of the entire hospital: financial planning, personnel,
medical activities, and plant.

1986 - 1987: Assistant Director, Vicksburg Community Hospitals.
Handled inpatient and outpatient admittance, cost control, and emergency
services.

1983 - 1986: Assistant Director, Plainwell Community Hospitals.
Managed billing practices, cost control, and new cost procedures.

COMMUNITY SERVICE

Volunteer Firefighter in Vicksburg, eight years.
Member of the committee to study the emergency care facilities in
Vicksburg.

RELEVANT INFORMATION

Participated in professional in-service seminars such as cost control,
financial planning, billing and collection systems, inpatient admittance, and
Lynn Hall's lecture series relating occupational therapy to the hospital
environment.

Member of the American Public Health Association and American Academy
of Hospital Administrators.

REFERENCES AVAILABLE

alfred d. landers

728 Bolero Court • Novato, CA 94945 • Alfred.Landers@xxx.com • (415) 555-2943

objective
To play an integral role on a pastoral care team in a hospital or mental health facility.

education
Training Center for Spiritual Directors, Taos Benedictine Abbey, NM, 2003
Intensive initiation into the art of spiritual direction.

Healing Ministries, Institute of Ministries, San Jose, CA, 2000–2003
Formation and advanced training, four semesters.

Clinical Pastoral Education, Mental Health, Western Coast Hospital, San Jose, CA, 1999–2001
Internship, four units.

pastoral experience
Community Member, Taos Benedictine Abbey, 2002–2003
Participated in counseling and prayer ministry with retreatants; participated in liturgies, retreats, and business office activities. Will complete training with an additional month-long program next year.

Chaplain Intern, Western Coast Hospital, 1999–2002
Pastoral focus on mentally ill offenders. Provided Eucharist ministry to patients in medical, surgical, neurological, geriatric, and adult psychiatric units. Participated in liturgy and prayer services. Provided pastoral interviews and counseling for people of various religious denominations and for nondenominational.

job history
Senior Commercial Lines Underwriter, Umbrella Insurance, Group Department, San Rafael, CA, 1989–present
Handle Oil Jobbers program in commercial group department, a nationwide program with heavy casualty, property, and inland marine coverage. Responsible for six states totaling in excess of $6 million in annual premiums. Implemented company changes in underwriting practices and procedures. Developed 10-step program for profit. Audit current files.

Personal Lines Underwriting Supervisor, Umbrella Insurance, San Rafael, CA, 1985–1993

Property and Casualty Underwriter, Umbrella Insurance, Newark, NJ, 1980–1985

References upon request

Arthur Lewis
789 Harborough Street • Boston, MA 02169
(617) 555-8962 • A.Lewis@xxx.com

Objective	To find employment in a human services field that offers new challenges and opportunities and utilizes my experience, skills, and knowledge from nearly 20 years of increasing responsibility in the education field

Specific Strengths

Creativity	ability to synthesize diverse ideas into coherent concepts, to think in new directions, and to assist others in more clearly stating their ideas and objectives
Tolerance	ability to work with a diverse population and enjoy the interaction and challenges of diversity; essentially team oriented and a people person
Assessment	ability to employ various standard and nonstandard assessment processes as well as mature insight in the evaluation of programs and proposals
Writing	ability to write informally and formally, imaginatively as well as in a scholarly, research-directed style
Speaking	ability to present challenging concepts in formal oral presentations
Teaching	significant ability with diverse student population; strong small group skills and experience

Education

M.A.	Education, 1988, University of Massachusetts, Boston, MA
B.A.	African American Studies and American Literature, 1985, Boston University, Boston, MA

Page 1 of 2

Employment History   Language Arts Department Head, Jamaica Plain
High School, Jamaica Plain, MA
2003–present
- Coordinate curriculum planning and
  implementation.
- Act as department liaison to school board and
  administration.
- Teach English, Creative Writing, Technical and
  Research Writing, American Literature, British
  Literature, and Multicultural Literature.
- Supervise the production and publication of a
  student literary magazine.

English and Writing Instructor, Jamaica Plain High
School, Jamaica Plain, MA
1995–2003
- Taught English, Creative Writing, Technical and
  Research Writing, American Literature, British
  Literature, Multicultural Literature, and Speech to
  high school students.
- Tutored remedial and advanced students of
  Literature and Writing.
- Served as faculty sponsor of African American
  Student Union.

Language Arts Instructor, Franklin Junior High
School, West Roxbury, MA
1990–1995
- Taught English, Reading, Speech, and Writing
  classes to seventh- and eighth-grade students.
- Faculty sponsor and advisor for the Student Drama
  Group.

Substitute Teacher, South Boston Districts, Boston,
MA
1988–1990
- Taught Language Arts classes in junior and senior
  high schools in South Boston.

References Available on Request

Hannah Bahirini

1610 Willow Lane • New Haven, KY 57220
H.Bahirini@xxx.com • (613) 555-1583

Position Desired: School Psychologist

Education: Williamshire University
                         Ed.S. School Psychology, 2001

                         Bellaire University
                         M.A. Psychology, 1992

                         North Salem University
                         B.A. Psychology, 1983

Certification: School Psychologist I

Work Experience: 6/00 to Present
                         Williamshire University Counseling and Testing Clinic
                         Position: Part-time Graduate Assistant

                         4/97 to 6/00
                         Kramer Clinic
                         Position: Addictions Counselor

                         12/93 to 4/97
                         Children's Services
                         Position: Counselor

                         11/88 to 12/93
                         Comp-tek, Inc.
                         Position: Office Manager

Memberships: Williamshire University Graduate Council
                         Office Held: Student Representative

                         Williamshire University Association of Graduate
                         Counselors
                         Office Held: Vice President

                         References available on request

Alexander Clarke
85 Starview Lane • Muncie, Indiana 47308
(765) 555-6812 • Alexander.Clark@xxx.com

Career Objective
Position as a health care administrator in a hospital
or clinic serving the mentally disabled.

Education
Ball State University, Muncie, Indiana
Bachelor of Science, June 1995
Major: Psychology
Minor: Accounting
Grades: 3.32/4.0 (major), 3.49/4.0 (overall)
Honors: Kappa Delta Tau (Honor Society in Psychology),
Dean's List (5 times)

Professional Experience
1/03 - Present
Managing Director, Craig L. Turner Clinic, Muncie, Indiana
• Direct operation of the clinic, which includes financial
planning, personnel, and cost control.
• Coordinate nursing and medical activities.

6/00 - 12/02
Assistant Director, Kelly Hospital, Indianapolis, Indiana
• Managed medical records department, inpatient
admittance, and budget planning.

7/96 - 5/00
**Administrative Supervisor, Muncie Community Hospitals,
Muncie, Indiana**
• Trained personnel, hired staff, and administered educational services.

References Available

Tucker Wendell

P.O. Box 12597
Portland, OR 97203
(503) 555-9041
Tucker.Wendell@xxx.com

Objective

To continue my work with young people in a position as a vocational counselor in a program involved with at-risk or disadvantaged youth.

Experience

- ❖ Hired and trained workers in a variety of positions with a food-processing company.
- ❖ Supervised high school–age workers in fast food restaurant.
- ❖ Served as volunteer coordinator of annual jobs fair for high school students.
- ❖ Coordinated with business people, professionals, and employers to develop a program directed to high school students for career planning and preparation.
- ❖ Assisted with summer camp and outdoor school programs for local school district.
- ❖ Taught woodworking segment at camp.
- ❖ Appointed president of the Parent-Teacher Association.

Skills

- ❖ Communicate well with a wide range of people.
- ❖ Knowledge of job training and hiring procedures.
- ❖ Understanding of work requirements and skills of teenage workers.
- ❖ Strong grasp of employer needs and expectations in local job market.
- ❖ Counsel students on job demands and opportunities.
- ❖ Developed contacts in the work world that could be invaluable to young people seeking job opportunities.
- ❖ Work with children of all ages, from elementary student campers to the students who work as camp counselors.
- ❖ Coordinate with parents to solve problems.

Employment

Employment and Training Manager, Food-Pac Corporation, Portland, OR, 2000–present.

❖ Hire and train line workers and shift supervisors in food-processing company.

❖ Work with local employment agencies and high school and college counselors to find qualified individuals for specialty assignments.

❖ Handle employee performance evaluations.

❖ Developed reporting system to monitor productivity and established reward program.

Manager, Burger King Corporation, Store #1252, 1990–2000.

❖ Hired and trained high school students and older workers for food preparation and cashier positions.

❖ Monitored sales reports.

❖ Scheduled shifts for more than 30 employees.

❖ Conducted employee performance reviews.

Education

Portland Community College, Portland, A.A. in Business, 2000.

References available upon request.

Sample Cover Letters

This chapter contains sample cover letters for students and graduates who are pursuing a wide variety of jobs and careers in social services.

There are many different styles of cover letters in terms of layout, level of formality, and presentation of information. These samples also represent people with varying amounts of education and work experience. Choose one cover letter or borrow elements from several different cover letters to help you construct your own.

Salvador Mendez

■ ■ ■

6413 North Sheridan Road, #2B • Chicago, Illinois 60626
(773) 555-8623 • Sal.Mendez@xxx.com

Ms. Kathryn Chambers   August 26, 20__
Human Resources
Rollins Family Center
206 North Kolmar Avenue
Chicago, IL 60624

Dear Ms. Chambers:

Kindly consider me an applicant for the position of Assistant Outreach Director as advertised in Sunday's *Chicago Tribune*. The enclosed resume outlines some of my qualifications for this job.

Your advertisement states that applicants should have a Master's degree in social work and at least three years of experience in individual and family therapy. In addition, you are looking for someone knowledgeable about substance and alcohol abuse and sensitive to the social and cultural needs of a diverse population. I believe you will find that my background matches these requirements.

I have three years' experience as a crisis intervention social worker at Lutheran General Hospital. Approximately one-third of the cases I have managed have been directly related to substance and/or alcohol abuse. As a doctoral student at the Institute for Clinical Social Work, I have focused my research on substance abuse and am currently preparing my manuscript, "Effective Psychotherapy for Substance Abusers," for publication. It includes 20 specific case studies with detailed long- and short-term counseling strategies as well as information regarding family and community support services.

The patients I counsel in the emergency room and medical clinic represent the diverse population of the Chicago area. I have concentrated my outreach involvement in the Hispanic community and have coordinated Lutheran General's efforts for early intervention therapy through the Howard Avenue Clinic. I am also familiar with the Rollins Family Center and the multicultural community it serves. I have consulted with several of your staff members, including Maria Gonzalez and Dr. Phillip Meyers, whose clients have been admitted to Lutheran General.

I would welcome the opportunity to meet with you to further discuss my qualifications for the position of Assistant Outreach Director. You can contact me at (773) 555-8623 or at (312) 555-3158. I look forward to hearing from you.

Respectfully,

Salvador Mendez

Elizabeth Anne Engle

16 N. Sheffield Rd.
Minneapolis, MN 55429
Liz.Engle@xxx.com
(612) 555-1423

March 21, 20__

Mr. Walter Howard
Director of Staff Development
St. Mary's Children's Hospital
2346 Bloomington Avenue
Minneapolis, MN 55404

Dear Mr. Howard:

I am writing in response to your recent advertisement in the *Minneapolis Star*. The position of Case Manager at St. Mary's Children's Hospital seems to be a perfect match to my career objectives, and my professional qualifications meet your requirements. I would appreciate the opportunity to discuss my credentials for this position with you during a personal interview.

Your ad states that you are seeking an M.S.N. with strong professional background in patient advocacy and family support services. As a Nursing Consultant for the past three years at Swedish-American Hospice, I have provided long-term assistance to more than 100 patients and their families. I designed the current program of family support services at the hospice that has been used as a model for three other long-term care centers in Minnesota. I supervise six patient advocates and provide mandatory training in the area of patients' rights to all new medical personnel at Swedish-American.

My experience as a pediatric staff nurse at Shriners Children's Hospital has made me sensitive to the particular needs of children and their families in times of medical crisis. I would welcome the chance to combine my nursing and advocacy skills in the field of pediatrics.

I can be reached on a confidential basis during the day at (612) 555-3674 or in the evenings at my home number at (612) 555-1423. Thank you for your consideration.

Sincerely,

Elizabeth Anne Engle

GREG SIMON

947 W. Harwood Road
Lawrenceburg, IN 47025
g.simon@xxx.com
(812) 555-5680

July 6, 20__

Mr. Robert Gilmore
Lawrenceburg Sports Club
1502 Prospect Drive
Lawrenceburg, IN 47025

Dear Mr. Gilmore:

My supervisor, Captain James Willes, suggested that I contact you regarding a possible opening for a firearms instructor at the Lawrenceburg Sports Club. I hope that after reviewing the enclosed resume you will agree that I have the training and professional dedication to qualify to teach at your club.

I have served honorably with the Lawrenceburg Police Department for two years. My firearms certifications include Special Weapons and Tactics and Indiana State Firearms Instructing. As an International Firearms Instructors Organization member, I meet with other police officers to discuss ways to improve firearms safety and education. I also help draft the organization's teaching guidelines. To date, I have led three firearms training courses.

I am dedicated to providing quality firearms instruction and am certain you share this goal. I would enjoy meeting with you to discuss the prospect of employment at the Lawrenceburg Sports Club and our mutual goal of firearms safety.

Sincerely,

Greg Simon

MICHELLE JUNG

28 Elm Street

Brockton, MA 02403

Michelle.Jung@xxx.com

(508) 555-6843

November 6, 20__

Ms. Joyce Maynard
Hillside Women's Correctional Center
18 Harris Street
Boston, MA 02109

Dear Ms. Maynard:

A mutual friend of ours, Roberta Sinclair, suggested that I contact you. Roberta was a student at Mount Holyoke College while I was the director of the college career center. I provided her with career counseling in her junior and senior years, and after graduation she returned to volunteer as my assistant. When I made the decision to open my own business, Roberta was chosen as my successor. Since then, we have remained close friends and colleagues. She tells me that you are looking for someone to conduct career-counseling seminars for inmates who are approaching release. I have enclosed my resume to give you an indication of my experience in this field and would appreciate the opportunity to meet with you to discuss my qualifications in more detail.

For the past five years, I have provided career counseling to more than 200 individuals. This has included assessing clients' career strengths, planning job search strategies, and motivating individuals to maximize their potential. I have counseled corporate groups as large as 250. When the Atlas Paper Company closed its Brockton plant in 1999 and had to lay off more than 100 employees, the director of personnel hired me to help these workers seek new jobs. I have also worked as a consultant for the United Standard Insurance Company and Brighton Business Associates.

I have a particular interest in helping women develop comprehensive plans for self-improvement through successful job placement. I have developed and presented seminars at the Grove Street Women's Center and the Brockton Community Center for women returning to the workforce.

I can be contacted at my office during business hours at (508) 555-6843 or by e-mail at michelle.jung@xxx.com. I am looking forward to speaking with you; Roberta has told me a great deal about you.

Sincerely,

Michelle Jung

allan a. mcfarlan

5448 W. Fournier Road
Westerly, RI 02891
Home: 401-555-4191
Cell: 401-555-0892
Email: Allan.McFarlan@xxx.com

March 16, 20__

Wilkes-Jacob Incorporated
64 Michigan Avenue
Washington, DC 20010

Dear Colleagues:

The reputation of Wilkes-Jacob Incorporated as a key provider of library services to the federal government has inspired me to investigate obtaining a position with your company. I am interested in putting my proven library skills to work in a setting where I can assist patrons with research projects and advance my professional growth. Please consider the enclosed resume for any current or future openings.

At Providence College I am responsible for a collection of 680,000 volumes housed in four separate libraries. During my tenure, 120,000 volumes have been added, and the cataloguing system has been updated and automated. I supervise a staff of five librarians, nine assistant librarians, and more than 30 students performing information retrieval using databases such as Dialog and Lexis.

I am planning to move to Washington, DC, next month and would enjoy discussing my qualifications with you when I arrive, or earlier should you have an immediate opening. I can be reached at (401) 555-4191 until April 26. After that, contact me at (703) 555-2164. Thank you for considering my credentials.

Sincerely,

Allan A. McFarlan

Mary A. Griffin

102 N. Edgewater Court ❱ Easton, PA 18042 ❱ M.Griffin@xxx.com
(215) 555-8815

November 2, 20__

Ms. Jane Kennedy
St. Clair Hospital
100 Bower Hill Road
Pittsburgh, PA 15243

Dear Ms. Kennedy:

I am seeking a position within a senior care center dedicated to meeting the needs
of the elderly. I understand that St. Clair Hospital is seeking an experienced public
relations specialist/fundraiser for part-time employment. After considering my resume,
I think you will agree that I am the right person for this job.

For 11 years as the director of the Easton Community Senior Center, I have been
responsible for all aspects of the center's operations. The center has more than 200
registered members, 5 full-time staffers, and 30 volunteers. During my tenure, I have
increased the budget by 80 percent, 90 percent of which came from grant proposals and fundraising activities. By publishing a monthly newsletter and articles for the
local newspapers, I have generated interest in and financial support of the center.
I also meet regularly with members of the Easton Business Association to solicit contributions for the center.

I would like the opportunity to present my portfolio and discuss specific fundraising
activities with you. I am sure my experiences at the Easton Senior Center could be
applied with the same positive results at St. Clair's Senior Center. Thank you for your
time and consideration.

Sincerely,

Mary A. Griffin

Janet K. Schafer
1026 River Road
Columbia, MO 65201

March 24, 20__

Michael Johnson, Personnel Department
St. Luke's Institute
6674 Beachview Drive
Columbia, MO 65203

Dear Mr. Johnson:

Enclosed please find my resume in response to your advertisement in the *Columbia Democrat* for a Social Worker/Psychotherapist. This position is very much in line with my current career objective, and I believe you will find my qualifications meet all of your requirements.

Your advertisement calls for a state-licensed social worker who has experience with substance abuse populations. From 2000 to 2003, I worked as an addiction therapist at Holy Cross Hospital. My responsibilities included assessing clients' needs, organizing comprehensive treatment plans, and developing educational programs and materials. In addition, I counseled family members in group sessions and provided individual treatment for adult children of alcoholics. During my two years as a crisis therapist at Boone Hospital Center, I have continued to work with clients with substance or alcohol addictions. Many of the crises I have encountered in the hospital emergency room are the result of alcohol and/or other substance abuse.

Although my work at the Boone Hospital Center has been challenging and rewarding, I am interested in working in a small psychiatric hospital as a member of an interdisciplinary treatment team. I would like to help develop program planning and to work with clients in a long-term, complete care addiction center.

Please contact me at my office, (314) 555-3786, or in the evenings at my home number, (314) 555-1678. I am anxious to discuss my background and the specifics of this position.

Sincerely,

Janet K. Schafer

CHRISTINA RIVERA

607 Ramsey Drive
Arlington, Virginia 22209
C.Rivera@xxx.com
(703) 555-2821

May 2, 20__

Lincolnwood Elementary School
P.O. Box 64
Richmond, Virginia 68712

Dear Colleagues:

I am extremely interested in the special education opening for next fall that you announced in last Sunday's *Richmond Gazette*. My skills and experience seem to be exactly what you seek to serve the special education students at Lincoln Elementary School.

I recently acquired my M.Ed. at the University of Virginia; the focus of my studies was learning disabilities and social/emotional disorders. Although my special education degree is newly acquired, I am not a beginner, since I have three years of experience as an elementary teacher. Please find the enclosed resume, which provides further details.

If it appears that my experience qualifies me for the position, I would appreciate a personal interview to discuss your needs and expand on my abilities in person. I can be reached in the evening at (703) 555-4991 or by e-mail at C.Rivera@xxx.com. Thank you for your consideration. I look forward to hearing from you.

Sincerely,

Christina Rivera

Sandra McQuiston

200 E. Third Avenue
St. Paul, MN 55415
sandy.mcquiston@xxx.com
(651) 555-4732

March 13, 20__

Marian Kelly
Kelly Career Consultants
1411 Main Street
Rockville, MD 20857

Dear Ms. Kelly:

I enjoyed meeting you last week at the NEVGA conference. Our conversation about your expanding private career-consulting practice has stayed with me. As you know, I gave up my own private practice to direct the Campus Counseling Center at College of St. Catherine. Although I enjoy my current position, the idea of returning to private practice is appealing. I would like to accept your offer to visit Rockville to discuss a possible position with your career-consulting firm.

As an experienced counselor and former owner of my own practice, I can appreciate both the joys and difficulties of an expanding practice. I feel qualified to assist you with that overload because my client base has been large and diverse enough to include everything from college seniors struggling with career options to corporate clients seeking outplacement services for displaced workers.

My enclosed resume expands on my qualifications. What it doesn't adequately convey is the energy and strong sense of professionalism I bring to my work. I hope you still feel ready to hire an associate because I think our skills and personalities would mesh well. I will call you next week to set up a meeting.

Sincerely,

Sandra McQuiston

THOMAS LUTHRA

33 Humphrey Street, Apt. 2B • Washington, DC 20059
Cell: (301) 555-0987 • Business: (301) 555-5347
Email: Tom.Luthra@xxx.com

May 14, 20__

Mr. David Rosenberg
American Federation for Academic Excellence
640 18th Street NW
Washington, DC 20006

Dear Mr. Rosenberg:

I am enclosing my curriculum vitae in response to your May 10th advertisement in the *Washington Post*. I believe the credentials I would bring to the position of Director of Research will interest you. As my vitae indicate, I have extensive academic counseling expertise, management skills, and public relations ability gained at universities in the United States and abroad.

In my present position as Director of the Career Planning Center at Howard University, I supervise a staff of nineteen and administer a career counseling and development program for Howard University students and faculty. I enjoy the challenge of providing pre-law counseling, designing career seminars, and assisting students with applications for graduate fellowships. Previously, I served the university for four years as Assistant Dean for Supportive Services. In that capacity I supervised a staff of seven, managed a budget of $900,000, and helped implement a university-wide tutoring program.

My experience at Howard University is only a small part of my academic background. Details of my teaching and consulting experience (gained at Missouri Southern State College, Northeastern University, Tehran English Language Institute, and York College) are included in my vitae. The vitae also provide information about recent publications and awards.

As a professional educator I have the highest respect for the contributions your organization makes to the advancement of higher education in the United States. I would welcome the opportunity to assist in that effort as your new Director of Research. I look forward to hearing from you.

Sincerely,

Thomas Luthra

JUAN MARTINEZ

2453 Cambridge Road
Kansas City, MO 64108
Cell Phone: (681) 555-8976
Email: juan.martinez@xxx.com

June 24, 20__

Mr. Rahmell Jackson
Association of Midwest Nurses
6418 Tanglewood Lane
Kansas City, MO 64108

Dear Mr. Jackson:

I was excited to learn, via your announcement in the *American Library Journal*, that the Association of Midwest Nurses is expanding its research library. After reviewing the enclosed resume, I hope that you will agree that I am highly qualified for the position of reference librarian at your facility.

Since receiving my M.L.S. from Rosary College in 2000, I have worked for Wright High School and as a librarian for the Kansas City Public Libraries. My supervisors value my work and enthusiasm and have witnessed my skill in the following areas:
• Budget development
• Materials acquisition
• Community outreach
• Staff training and supervision

If you feel a personal interview is appropriate, I am available at your convenience. You may reach me on my cell phone at (681) 555-8976, or on a confidential basis at work, (681) 555-6435. I am looking forward to your reply.

Respectfully,

Juan Martinez

MILTON R. ROSENBURG

650 Second Street • Portland, OR 97204

M.Rosenburg@xxx.com • (503) 555-6418

February 2, 20__

Mr. David Elkin, Director
Cheney Community Center
750 Green Street
Tacoma, WA 98447

Dear Mr. Elkin:

As social service professionals, we understand the devastating effect of substance abuse on our communities. In my work as a counselor at the Portland Mental Health Center, I face the challenge of assisting substance abusers every day. I would like to relocate to Tacoma and am hoping there may be room on the staff at Cheney for a counselor with my expertise.

In addition to my counseling background, I have both a degree and experience in the field of leisure and recreation. I planned and created the Seattle Community Recreation Center in 1995 to provide guidance and supervised activities for local youth. Previous to that I was the Student Activities Director at Pacific Lutheran University in Tacoma.

If this combination of recreational and counseling skills seems a match for your current needs, you may reach me at (503) 555-6418 to discuss my qualifications further or arrange a personal interview. Thank you for your consideration.

Yours truly,

Milton R. Rosenburg

■ ■ ■ ANN OLIVERA ■ ■ ■

664 E. Ivy Drive
Nashville, TN 37212
615/555-4573

July 11, 20__

Ms. Indira Suresh
Adoption Services Coordinator
Belmont Child and Family Services
16 S. Belmont Road
Nashville, TN 37212

Dear Ms. Suresh:

Your colleague Martha Baylor has encouraged me to write to you regarding a possible position at Belmont Child and Family Services as an adoptions caseworker. I currently work at Greater Nashville Social Services, where I supervise an adoptions intake unit with a staff of four. The enclosed resume explains my experience in the fields of adoption, child custody, veterans' affairs, psychiatric crisis intervention, and domestic violence.

Both my experience and client base have been diverse, which enables me to handle complex and emotionally charged social service cases with relative ease. My commitment to my profession is strong, as the references listed on my resume will attest. Continued education is essential in our work, and I strive to stay abreast of both legal issues and current theory on adoption. One of my strengths is my ability to empathize with all parties in adoption and custody cases and understand the needs and rights of both biological parents and adoptive families.

If I can provide further information about my credentials, please feel free to contact me at home at 615/555-4573 or at work at 615/555-8100. I would enjoy meeting with you at your convenience to discuss the fine work you do at Belmont.

Sincerely,

Ann Olivera